Women as
Educational Leaders

Dedicated to Alana, Heather, and Felisha

Marie Somers Hill
Joyce C. Ragland

Women as Educational Leaders

Opening Windows, Pushing Ceilings

CORWIN PRESS, INC.
A Sage Publications Company
Thousand Oaks, California

For information address:

Corwin Press, Inc.
A Sage Publications Company
2455 Teller Road
Thousand Oaks, California 91320

SAGE Publications Ltd.
6 Bonhill Street
London EC2A 4PU
United Kingdom

SAGE Publications India Pvt. Ltd.
M-32 Market
Greater Kailash I
New Delhi 110 048 India

Printed in the United States of America

Library of Congress Cataloging-in-Publication Data

Hill, Marie Somers.
    Women as educational leaders: opening windows, pushing ceilings /
authors, Marie Somers Hill, Joyce C. Ragland.
        p. cm.
    Includes bibliographical references and index.
    ISBN 0-8039-6136-7 (cloth: acid-free paper). — ISBN
0-8039-6137-5 (pbk.: acid-free paper)
        1. Women school administrators—United States—Interviews.
    2. Women educators—United States—Interviews. 3. Educational
    leadership—United States. I. Ragland, Joyce C. II. Title.
    LB2831.62.H55 1995
    371.2'0082—dc20   94-46410

This book is printed on acid-free paper.

95 96 97 98 99 10 9 8 7 6 5 4 3 2 1

Corwin Press Production Editor: Diane S. Foster

Contents

Preface   ix

About the Authors   xiii

Part I: Women Leaders and the New Reality   1

1. Understanding the Baggage of the Past   5
      Contemporary Educational Leadership   6
      Baggage From Historical Myths and
            Cultural Expectations   7
      Dumping the Baggage   16

2. Seizing the Catalysts of Today   17
      Administrative Demographics   18
      Messiahs, Scapegoats, and Sacrificial Lambs   20
      Extended Visions of Possibilities   22
      Expanding Leadership Dimensions in Schooling   23

More Comfortable Graduate School Settings 25
Changed Internal Influences 28
Final Thoughts 29

3. **Envisioning the Future** 31
Predictions 32
Potential Downsides 36
Health Issues 37

Part II: Strategies for Professional and Self-Development 39
Highlights of Legislation, Events, Publications
Important to Women Leaders 40
A Sample Process for Breaking the Glass Ceiling 41

4. **Developing and Assessing Our Leadership Competency** 43
New Influences on Concepts of Leadership 45
Categorizing Traps 47
Growing Through Self-Assessment 49
Strategies to Strengthen Leadership Skills 50
Considering Hardiness 51
Summary 55
Appendix: Self-Assessment of Leadership
Competencies 55
Summation of Self-Assessment 61

5. **Learning From Pathfinders** 63
Education 64
Rewards: Intrinsic and Extrinsic 66
Stick-to-itivity 68
Support Systems 70
Varia 71

6. **Recognizing Mentoring Reciprocals** 72
Mentoring 72
Learning Organizational Nuances 73
Reciprocal Benefits 74
Mentoring: An Essential for Women's Professional
Development 75

Challenges With Gender Dimensions   77
Mentoring as Part of the Organizational Culture   78
Stages of Mentorship Relationships   81
Strategies for Finding a Mentor   83
Possible Mentor Candidates   84
Final Thoughts   84

7. **Developing Networks**   **87**
Networking's Fit With Now   88
Overcoming the Historical Culture of Isolation   88
Ways to Create Networks in Schools and
    School Systems   89
Strategies for Personal Networking   97
Final Thoughts   99

8. **Exploring Paths**   **101**
Degree Paths of Interviewees   102
Educational Paths of Interviewees   103
Early Work Experience   103
Career Paths in Education   104
Would They Do It All Again?   105
Mobility Issues   106
Issues of Child Care   106
Sacrifices   107
Gender Bias?   107
Leisure Activities   109
The Superwoman Syndrome?   109
Addendum: Planned Affirmative Action   110
Conclusion   111

References   **113**

Suggested Readings   **123**

Index   **125**

Preface

"Women and minorities are encouraged to apply."

Job announcements for leadership positions routinely reflect a growing awareness of the need to hire women and minorities to become part of the leadership team. In the past two decades, the number of women in educational administration has been steadily increasing. Yet, when attending national conferences with agendas of several hundred presentations, the dearth of information about the contributions and practice of women in public school administration becomes startlingly obvious. Little literature focuses on women leaders in education. The theoretical bases of educational leadership are overwhelmingly established on research generated by white males studying white male leaders. Research studies reveal a field still dominated by men but with increasing numbers of women. Now that the landscapes of educational leadership reflect expanded hues, philosophies, and another gender, newly formulated as well as replicated research is needed to balance the picture. Our goal is not to discard the present body of literature but to incorporate new understandings, open new possibilities, and highlight new successful structures.

This book is based on a series of interviews of women leaders identified as outstanding by other educators, male and female. The women interviewed share experiences from their personal and professional lives and candidly reveal their frustrations, insights, and strategies for advancement. This is not a theory-based book but a practitioner's guide, if you will, for women who aspire to leadership positions in educational settings.

The Introduction to Part I outlines procedures used for conducting 35 interviews of selected women educational leaders. To strengthen perspective regarding the range of experience and depth of quality within the interviews, each interviewee's name and affiliation is listed.

Chapter 1, "Understanding the Baggage of the Past," explores traditional roadblocks to the advancement of women in educational administrative roles. Barriers are discussed in the context of six main themes, including the long-standing male dominance of key leadership positions; women's historically scarce political savvy, career positioning, mentoring, and visibility; and, finally, the general internal barriers and bias that women, themselves, maintain. The chapter focuses on "dumping" old myths, stereotypes, barriers, and baggage.

Chapter 2, "Seizing the Catalysts of Today," emphasizes the optimal convergence of a variety of factors that allow women today to assume increasingly important positions as decision makers and gatekeepers within every level of education. Six catalysts assembling to create new vistas for women in educational leadership encompass favorable administrative demographics; taking advantage of imposed roles as messiahs, scapegoats, or sacrificial lambs; extended visions of possibilities; expanded roles in schooling; more comfortable graduate school settings; and changed internal influences.

Chapter 3, "Envisioning the Future," discusses trends in the near future for women in the ranks of educational administration as envisioned by the interviewees.

Part II, "Strategies for Professional and Self-Development," includes five chapters of research-based and interviewee advice from their own experiences for securing and excelling in educational leadership positions.

The first chapter of Part II, Chapter 4, "Developing and Assessing Our Leadership Competency," contains a self-assessment instrument and a plan for developing one's leadership competencies. The chapter also provides information needed for examining one's hardiness levels.

In Chapter 5, "Learning From Pathfinders," the interviewees give their "gut-level advice" on the formal and informal structures leading to advancement in educational leadership arenas. They also provide advice on setting goals, noting the rewards encountered along the way.

Chapter 6, "Recognizing Mentoring Reciprocals," examines and offers advice on cultivating valuable mentoring relationships.

Techniques for extending interpersonal relationships are outlined further in Chapter 7, "Developing Networks." This chapter explores the essential nature of growing personally and professionally through a wide variety of contacts. Specific strategies are outlined for developing networks within new settings.

The final chapter, Chapter 8, "Exploring Paths," delves into the individual career paths of the women interviewees. National "norms" are compared.

This book contains guidelines, strategies, techniques, and common sense advice for enhancing the paths of women at any point in pursuing a career in educational leadership. The authors welcome your reactions to the findings as well as your personal insights as you open new doors and push old ceilings.

MARIE SOMERS HILL
East Tennessee State University

JOYCE C. RAGLAND
Northeast Missouri State University

About the Authors

Marie Somers Hill is Associate Professor in the Department of Educational Leadership and Policy Analysis at East Tennessee State University. She has held professorships at the University of Central Florida and Wesleyan College, was a guest lecturer at the University of the Yucatan, and was a principal and teacher for 16 years. Her first book was *Creating Safe Schools* (1994, Sage). Her articles have been published in many professional journals, including *NASSP Bulletin*, *Principal*, and the *Journal of School Leadership*, as well as in *Psychology Today*. She serves as a correspondent for *DESIGN for Leadership* and is on the editorial board of *Research in the Schools*.

She has conducted professional development workshops throughout the country for Phi Delta Kappa and various school districts. Her academic interests include leadership preparation programs and teacher leadership. She received her undergraduate degree from Glenville State College and her graduate degrees from Rollins College and Mississippi State University. She has completed postdoctoral studies at Vanderbilt University and the University of Alaska.

Joyce C. Ragland is Coordinator of Field Experiences at Northeast Missouri State University where she is an Associate Professor and Chief Certification Officer. In addition, she serves as the principal/director of the NMSU—Kirksville public school summer program for at-risk students, Grades 6 through 12. She has been an Assistant Professor at the University of Saskatchewan and at East Tennessee State University, where she was also Director of Student Teaching. She has served as a consultant in the critical thinking program in-service for public schools for the State of Illinois and has over 10 years' teaching experience in public schools.

Her areas of expertise include administrative theory, curriculum, critical thinking skills programs, and kindergarten through 12th-grade teaching strategies. She holds a doctorate in instructional process from Southern Illinois University at Edwardsville. Additional degrees include an education specialist degree in education administration, also from SIUE, an MA in education administration from Northeast Missouri State University, and a BA in music from College of the Ozarks. Additional graduate course work includes studies at the University of Missouri at Columbia, the University of Missouri at Kansas City, and the Institute of European Studies in Vienna, Austria.

PART I

Women Leaders and the New Reality

In public school leadership, many outstanding women have attained positions of importance through a series of jobs, often being the first woman to serve in some capacities. Thirty-five women were interviewed to determine their gathered insights as well as their predictions for the future. The interviews often revealed pleasant surprises. Many of their experiences, impressions, and opinions support the established literature. Some do not.

Each woman was interviewed by one of the two authors. Women were selected because they each started their educational careers as classroom teachers, then moved along 35 different routes to positions as superintendents, school board members, principals, and school officials at national, state, and local levels. From these public school administrative positions, many have now moved to related businesses or positions in higher education.

Interviews began with a small number of women recognized as exceptional in their present positions. At the end of each interview, participants nominated others who should be interviewed in a snowball technique. Attempts were made to interview many other women, but because of demanding schedules, some were unavailable for interviewing within the time frame of this study. Far more

1

women who have made, and are making, exceptional contributions to educational leadership could have been interviewed.

Providing a sample of women's perspectives from a representative geographic area was a priority of this study. Consequently, women were interviewed from 19 states and 2 provinces. Experiences of these educational leaders represent rural, suburban, and urban school districts with common and disparate challenges. Women of color and women varying in age from their 30s to their 60s are represented in our sample.

The outstanding women interviewed for this book include the following:

Marsha Barrett
Principal
Blue Valley High School
Stillwell, KS

Bonnie Baum
Superintendent
Colfax-Mingle District
Colfax, IA

Judy Blitch
Division Chair
Wesleyan College
Macon, GA

Mary Jane Connelly
Department Head
University of Tennessee
Knoxville, TN

Ann Cuzzola
School Board Member and
    Department Chair
Mercy Hurst Preparatory
    School
Erie, PA

Gina Decker
Managing Editor and Senior
    Consultant
Community Collaborators
Charlottesville, VA

Rose Dillard
Superintendent
Mid-Prairie Community District
Wellman, IA

Frances Disselhorst
Principal
Horace Mann Middle School
Burlington, IA

Celestine Ferguson
Assistant Commissioner of
    Education
Department of Elementary and
    Secondary Education
Jefferson City, MO

Leslie Ford
Vice President for Product Development and Editor in Chief
Steck Vaughan Publishing Co.
Austin, TX

Debbie Garland
Assistant Principal
Edwardsville High School
Edwardsville, IL

Lois Gray
Superintendent
Hardin County Schools
Elizabethton, KY

Patricia Henley (former super-
 intendent)
Elementary Principal
Ft. Osage RI District
Independence, MO

Marilyn Herr
Principal
Andover Elementary School
Andover, KS

Jean Hill
Director of Instruction
Bristol City Schools
Bristol, VA

Sandra Hill
High School Vice-Principal
Prince Albert School
Assiniboia, Saskatchewan

Patsy Johnson
Assistant Professor
University of Alabama
University, AL

Janet Johnston
Assistant Superintendent[1]
Battle River School District
Lloydminster, Alberta

JoAnn Krueger
Director of Administrative
 Internship Programs
University of New Mexico
Albuquerque, NM

Jane Lindle
Associate Professor
University of Kentucky
Lexington, KY

Nancy Livesay
Project Director
SouthEastern Regional Vision
 for Education
Tallahassee, FL

Altha Manning
Commissioner of Human
 Resource Development
Tallahassee, FL

Shari Marshall
Superintendent
Smithton CC
Smithton, IL

Ruth Ann Marston
Principal
Herrera Elementary School
Phoenix, AZ

Charlene Morita
Director of Child Development
 Programs
San Juan Unified District
Carmichael, CA

Jane Page
Department Chair
Georgia Southern University
Statesboro, GA

Bobby Jo Peters
Staff Development Facilitator
Virginia Department of
Education

Joni Powers
Principal
Colt Andrews School
Bristol, RI

Jahala Rohner
Assistant Principal
Blue Springs South High School
Blue Springs, MO

Dorothy Routh
Director
Education Enhancement
Florida State University
Tallahassee, FL

Petra Snowden
Graduate Program Director
Old Dominion University
Virginia Beach, VA

Gail Williams
Superintendent
Lee's Summit RVII
Lee's Summit, MO

Linda Wesson
Associate Professor
Arkansas State University
State University, AR

Annette Wilson
Instructor
Appalachian State University
Boone, NC

Carol Whitehead
Assistant Superintendent for
Curriculum and Instruction/
    Staff Development
Tacoma, WA

An interview protocol was established to ensure greater consistency in the process and to "make sure that essentially the same information is obtained from a number of people by covering the same material" (Patton, 1987, p. 111). Following initial construction of the protocol, it was tested with 22 female graduate students. Their comments subsequent to commencing the interviews resulted in more concise wording.

The remainder of Part I describes historical and cultural legacies that have surrounded women in educational leadership. Present conditions that provide optimum timing for the advancement of women through the ranks of educational leadership are also explored.

Note

1. Assistant superintendent is the title in the United States corresponding to assistant director in Canadian schools.

1

Understanding the
Baggage of the Past

Because of their increasing numbers in the professional workplace, more and more frequent encounters and interactions occur with women in roles as police officers, physicians, lawyers, sportswriters, and a variety of other careers. Higher percentages of working women are represented not only in the professions but also in other high-paying jobs with extensive responsibility and authority. As more women attain these professional positions, their influence extends. Aburdene and Naisbitt (1992) found that women, in following new paths and reaching new horizons, are really building new realities. New realities cause us all to rethink and redefine long-held cultural mores.

Contemporary Educational Leadership

Cracks in the male-controlled educational leadership estab-lishment are also beginning to appear. Opportunities for women to assume leadership positions within educational communities are now available. Although the percentages are still small, the number of women superintendents and principals increased throughout the 1980s and into the 1990s. Sustained increases seem possible due to steadily increasing percentages of women making up the ranks of potential administrators seeking graduate degrees in leadership preparation programs.

Because of complexities within our contemporary culture, im-ages and expectations of leaders have changed. Nowhere are com-plexities and new expectations more evident than in education. Schools and schooling have taken on the ills of our entire society. If there is a problem, education is expected to fix it. After years of responsibility solely for academic needs, schools now handle health, welfare, and family responsibilities. If no one in the home will teach or model responsibility and values, schools assume the job. If no one is available to baby-sit, the school opens from 6 a.m. to 10 p.m. If the family needs help, from marital counseling to financial assistance, the school becomes the hub for services. If the community is stran-gled in violence, the school strives to provide a safe haven and a center for mediation. The school as a microcosm of the community is shouldering the community's problems in ever changing patterns (Hill & Hill, 1994). These responsibilities create difficult and chal-lenging times for educators, especially for leaders. The different di-mensions of our problems have compounded and interwoven to the point that either leaders must be superhuman or they must become skilled at pulling together resources, whether financial or human. Circumstances surrounding leadership today demand that we shed stereotypical images and seek leaders who are competent in foster-ing talents of others and skilled at unifying constituencies to address problems.

Because of immediate needs to find competent educational leaders, all segments of society must be considered to find the very best. The female half of our population has often been ignored, ridi-culed, thwarted, or prevented from considering leadership roles. To begin changing this precedent, we will consider what baggage must be understood for women to move forward as leaders. With an understanding of this baggage, we can then pack it away and continue to move forward unburdened.

Baggage From
Historical Myths and Cultural Expectations

In spite of promising demographical statistics, equal opportunities for women to secure positions and advance in educational leadership are still hampered by some historical myths and contemporary barriers. As a necessary step to achieve success, the baggage of the past must be examined to find individual and gender-specific ways to progress.

Historical Myths as Barriers

Since groups of people have existed, women have been leaders. Even in prehistoric settings, when superior physical strength usually equated with leadership, women inadvertently led, controlled, and influenced others (see, e.g., Eisler, 1987). Circumstance and mental abilities afforded women early opportunities to lead. Most steps marking societal progress, including agriculture, trading, domesticating animals, establishing communities, and early construction, were developed by prehistoric women (Valiant, 1978). From her first novel, *The Clan of the Cave Bear,* Jean Auel (1980) produced a series of fictional chronicles of a cave age heroine. Auel's anthropological research produces a plausible saga demonstrating possibilities for early female leadership. The immense popularity of the series demonstrates a thirst still existing for such possibilities. Conflicts between the role of leader and expectations for female roles have occurred throughout history and in most cultures. In our own culture, we often find a view of women leaders weighed down by distorted images and stereotypes. Historical and contemporary myths full of icy virgins, fiery temptresses, and silent martyrs still encumber female leadership visions and possibilities in many ways.

For centuries, royalty was the only visible and legislatively possible female leadership role. The few women who ascended to the throne did so as a result of a default opportunity for leadership because a male heir was not available. In the interest of devoting their life to the realm, heroic queens were sometimes even expected to retain their virginity, such as Elizabeth I of England who had tragic relationships with men.

Other images of women as leaders include scenes of women scheming, gold digging, and seducing their way to the top. The unbalanced tabloid space currently devoted to a few unscrupulous women leaders (e.g., Imelda Marcos, Leona Helmsley) distorts images for all women. These stories generally portray devious and immoral women running over everyone in their way.

Perhaps no one invention has influenced North American mores more than television. Its arrival chronicled and reflected images and expectations of women. Betty Cleaver mediated for Beaver and the other men in her life while she did the ironing in her pearls and pumps. Kitty silently managed the saloon and town difficulties on *Gunsmoke*. Edith Bunker was ridiculed, embarrassed, and silenced as she tried to cover and solve the messes Archie created. This contrasting myth of martyrs conveys women sacrificing everything for the good of the cause with silent suffering preferred.

Unfortunately, many of today's television images of women are equally distorted. With only a few wonderful exceptions, women in leadership roles are disproportionately portrayed on television as manipulative, adversarial, bitchy, and distasteful. When the models of minority women are considered separately, images are even worse. Hispanic women are often "cha cha chicks" in red and ruffles, screaming with continual hysteria through life. African American women are frequently represented as fat and bossy or thin and dressed like hookers.

An additional stereotype of female leadership exists specifically for women in education. Traditionally, women in the field of education in North America were unmarried, harsh prudes. These undesirable women lived their lives through their school existence. Decades of rules and regulations prescribed every aspect of female educators' behavior, from the number of petticoats they must wear to their church attendance to permissible social engagements. Unless they survived off their father's largesse, they were also impoverished because the "divine calling" nature of the occupation justified their receiving meager salaries. Women were allowed leadership roles in education as long as they accepted the responsibility with none of the authority. The highest paying leadership roles were, and often still are, reserved for men, with subtleties not in duties but in job titles that serve to differentiate pay.

From Attila the Hun to Hitler to Jim Jones, men have also had negative leadership images to overcome. Men, however, have had the advantage of a wider range and larger numbers of images from which to select. Men's leaders have also prospered from excellent marketing campaigns and public expectation that because they are male, they are probably already competent. Societally, much of our thinking about leadership has not progressed far from assuming that the tallest man would naturally be the best leader.

Cultural Expectations as Barriers

Several barriers have created an educational system in which, historically, few women held leadership positions. Not only do many types of interwoven barriers exist, but, more imposing, they are maintained from multiple sources. These barriers include the following:

- Male dominance of key leadership positions
- Lack of political savvy
- Lack of career positioning
- Lack of mentoring
- Lack of mobility
- Internal barriers and bias against women

Male Dominance of Key Leadership Positions. This presents a significant barrier for women moving into roles as educational leaders. Traditionally, men have controlled the highest administrative jobs within school districts. Long-standing bureaucratic values have thwarted women's entering administration. Control was largely maintained by limiting change. The "system" fostered selection of new administrators who resembled their sponsors in attitude, philosophy, deed, and, even in many cases, appearance, hobbies, church affiliation, and club membership. In addition, successors were expected to mirror tightly defined concepts of administrative competency. Such a selection process resulted in the new mimicking the old down to nuances of behavior (Marshall & Mitchell, 1989).

In 1982, 1.8% of superintendencies in the United States were held by women. Although progress is evident, women had assumed only 3.7% of superintendencies by 1988 (Pigford & Tonnsen, 1993). Political control has been accomplished by male dominance not only in superintendencies but also in school board positions, professional associations, and unions. These positions provide economic as well as political power because they are primarily held by men earning four or five times what teachers, primarily female, earn.

In its role of training chief school executives, the university has for years been an example of a closed fraternity. Traditionally, faculty members in educational leadership departments have been male. This dominance has influenced career paths and choices of women in many ways. First, university faculty members initially encourage or discourage prospective graduate students about pursuing a degree. Once admitted to a program, faculty members foster and mentor future leaders. Finally, in many regions of the country, departments play central roles in selecting or at least nominating candidates for leadership roles.

The extent of the perception of men as gatekeepers is apparent in Mims's 1992 study of Georgia female educational leadership graduate students. Of the women in her study, 81% felt that males were favored in principalship selection. Of the women in Edson's 1987 study, 75% felt that their gender hindered advancement in educational administration. In a West Virginia survey, 55% of women who had completed principal preparation programs indicated that gender bias in hiring and promoting practices prevented them from acquiring administrative positions (Martin & Grant, 1990). Men with less teaching experience and fewer graduate hours were repeatedly selected over female candidates. Even when they finally did receive interviews, women in the West Virginia survey reported experiences with gender bias, such as being asked about how they could juggle an administrative job while simultaneously raising their children.

Faced with negative environments for advancement, many competent women seek other more enlightened avenues for their careers. When opportunities in other professions exist, overt discrimination in education becomes the force driving scores of women away. We cannot afford this loss of talent.

Lack of Political Savvy. This has also prevented women from moving forward in administrative positions. With men dominating gatekeeping, deals are often made and agreements cut before many women know positions are available. Many times, competent women with stronger qualifications are not considered. Understandings have already been bargained during golf, on the fishing trip, on the basketball court, or at the club. Women are not usually privy to those venues or to decisions made outside the work setting.

People in positions of power not only frequently decide finalists for other positions, but they also quite often determine their own successors. The "good ol' boy" network exists so strongly in many school districts that many men can tell you their number in line to the superintendency. They are just waiting their turn.

To benefit both children and the quality of education within their state, a few legislative bodies or state departments of education have been courageous enough to take on the good ol' boy network. Established policies require districts to demonstrate that leadership positions are filled with the most competent persons. These requirements can be cumbersome and demand extensive reporting and procedures for compliance. With extensive subterfuge, such regulation can be circumvented but not as easily as when no policy of accountability exists for hiring based on competency.

Lack of Career Positioning. Positioning is clearly discriminatory in job announcements requesting qualifications that women cannot meet because of closed ranks. For instance, a job application might require district or central office experience in a line position (traditionally male) rather than a staff position (traditionally female). One interviewee recalled a job announcement for a principalship requiring high school coaching experience.

Coaching, a background of high school teaching, and expertise in finance and negotiation have been nearly mandatory prerequisites for career paths of educational leaders to the highest levels. What usually happens is that selected "golden boys" or "young turks" are carefully positioned on the "right" district committees with the right people. They then are groomed to meet demands and specifications that they will face further along in their career.

Often, women have been denied those experiences and, generally, have not assertively sought or recognized those routes. Lack of mentoring may have led to a lack of anticipatory career positioning for many women. The gap and limited scope of the right experiences necessary to gain a superintendency, for instance, have hurt women's chances. Glass ceilings have been easily installed and maintained.

In addition, the scope of women's career responsibilities has limited their prospect for advancement. Although essential for sound educational programs, curricular and instructional dimensions of schools, predominantly left to women, have become career albatrosses. Those positions often restrict contact of women with policymakers.

Information regarding monies surrounding any job translates into power. Mystery, jargon, and purposeful complications restrict the understanding of budgets. Budget priorities, oversight, and, certainly, participation are often consciously withheld. Strangely, in many systems, budgets drive the curriculum rather than the reverse. This situation has forced instructional supervisors to make decisions on what are the best teaching practices and learning environments under the constraints of a budget determined elsewhere. In one more way, women often remain outside the decision-making loop.

Similar discrimination exists in educationally related fields. T. became the first female regional sales manager in a textbook publishing company. She had successfully held the job of sales representative, spending most of her time visiting schools, leading staff development, and talking with teachers about textbooks. After 6 years in the sales manager position, T. is still expected to conduct staff development and visit schools as well as do her managerial tasks. This expectation is not the same for male sales managers.

Job labels have also hurt advancement. For instance, in district offices, women will often be called "supervisors," whereas men with similar duties receive titles such as "director" or "associate superintendent." Titles structure pay scales and predict or prevent future advancement.

Traditionally, titles that are more commonly held by women than by men receive less pay. For instance, historically, deans of colleges of education have been more likely to be women than other deanships. Usually, they are the lowest paid deans on campuses. Similarly, in educational publishing, vice presidents of product development (the old curriculum and instruction albatross again) receive less pay than do vice presidents of finance, sales, or marketing. To achieve equity of pay and opportunity, increased awareness of proper positioning along a career path is necessary.

Lack of Mentoring. Mentoring to increase women's political savvy and career positioning know-how has been lacking for a variety of reasons. In certain cases, potential male mentors did not consider that women would want to lead or were interested in leading. In some organizations, cross-gender mentoring was discouraged because the relationship held the potential for being misunderstood as something more than career support.

Women in influential positions have also failed to mentor women for several reasons. Many pioneer female leaders lacked understandings of the power and processes of mentoring behavior.

In carving their own paths, women in certain educational areas or in specific school districts did not/do not have the time or did not recognize the value of a mentoring role in the scope of their careers. Furthermore, if a woman views herself as a token in a position of authority, she purposefully mentors no one. Regardless of her capability, a self-perceived token will be too threatened to foster leadership in others.

Women in our study discussed a common thread of feeling that they were "the only one" throughout their career. Because they were socially unacceptable or misunderstood, they guarded their feelings of ambition and drive. They learned that it was prudent to keep their ideas to themselves. Many exemplary women leaders have solitarily created a path and are just now discovering the concomitant gains of mentoring others. (Note: Recommendations surrounding mentoring roles can be found in Chapter 6.)

Lack of Mobility. When the employee is a single parent, mobility is a much bigger consideration for women than for men. Problems associated with being alone in a new setting are more significant for single women than for single men due to safety, socialization, and child care factors. Some women have also not moved to ensure more stability for their children's schooling or to maintain a support base of extended family or friends helping with child rearing.

Often, married women have elected not to move to protect their husbands' position, which in the past generally commanded a higher income. Over half of the women interviewed in our study had their career or graduate study interrupted or limited by a husband's career moves or the lack of his ability to move due to his job. Several interviewees recalled moves to four states. Another moved 14 times in 21 years. Many women interviewed recalled losing good jobs with promising promotions on the horizon to relocate somewhere else and become a substitute teacher.

This view and expectation of sacrifice is different for most men. A sample of Ph.D. economists found that 60% of the married women versus 25% of the men considered their spouse's mobility a problem and consideration in their own career development (Reagan, 1975). Earnings influence the power balance in households. Power is shifting due to increasingly higher salaries earned by women. In two-paycheck homes, 29% of the women earn more than their husbands. Furthermore, 85% of female senior executives earn more than their husbands. Although being the primary breadwinner instead of the bread maker means that they have increased involvement in spending and other household issues, women often work hard at keeping their superior incomes a secret (Sandroff, 1994). It will be interesting to see how quickly the phenomenon of wives giving up their careers for their husband's might change. Glimpses of the changing custom were seen when a few of the women participating in our interviews had experienced husbands following them to a new work location. One women noted that she and her husband took turns moving for each other's career.

Lack of mobility is often not even accurately identified by women as limiting career options. Mims (1992) asked Georgia female graduate students if they were willing to be mobile to secure a job. Fifty-seven percent said that they were. But when they were asked to clarify their concept of mobility, only 5% were willing to relocate beyond 100 miles, 10% would move out of their state for a position, and 36% would not go more than 50 miles. Another study (Edson, 1987) found a slightly larger acceptance of mobility by women; 75% were willing to leave their district, with 40% willing to leave the state.

The mobility consideration may also hinder female job advancement if organizations with vacancies assume that women cannot or will not move. They may not approach or even offer an interview to a preferred woman candidate if they assume she will decline a necessary move.

Internal Barriers and Bias Against Women. Yeakey, Johnston, and Adkison (1986) report that "discrimination is as deceptively complex as it is pervasively subtle" (p. 111). Discrimination against women exists in every culture to varying degrees of intent, severity, cruelty, and damage. Historically and globally, classifying groups as inferior and weak has been comforting and satisfying to the self-image of others. However, as with any other discrimination, entire cultures suffer due to the loss of potential talents and contributions of the group being stifled.

Findings in a study of female higher education administrators in Florida ring true to women in other settings. Study participants identified barriers to their advancement as numerous subtle biases. For instance, they recalled examples of being ignored during important discussions, interrupted when attempting to make a point, and dismissed through references that indicate or assume that a male really was the one to complete a solid project or make a successful decision (Stokes, 1984). The women further indicated less access to power through lack of invitations to dinners or golf matches where decisions or alliances were often made. Participants in this study felt that women had to work harder than men to succeed and to overcome biases.

Patterns of low expectation begin very early with the school experience of many girls. Studies by the American Association of University Women (AAUW, 1992) and compilations of research by Sadker, Sadker, and Klein (1991) highlight the gender bias existing in our schools at all levels. Female students are not just unevenly treated; they are harassed and abused by their male peers and by school personnel according to Shakeshaft and Cohan (1990). Early, consistent treatment conveying the message that females are less deserving and less worthy erodes self-esteem with lifelong effects.

Internal barriers keep women from advancing in their educational careers. Barriers range from a personal lack of confidence to a fear of challenging the cultural expectations of their role. A study of Canadian school administrators by Brathwaite in 1986 attributed lack of female advancement through district ranks as stemming largely from their oversaturation with the cultural message of female inferiority within white male systems.

Occasionally, women play a destructive game of using fragile images. Projecting weakness is sometimes a ploy by women seeking acceptance. Wolf (1994) coined the term *power feminism* to alert women to the dangers of claiming feminine specialness. For the benefit of excellence in education and on a larger scale for the future of the planet, equality must be demanded on the basis of human worth.

Dumping the Baggage

Barriers to women's advancement in administrative ranks are entrenched societal concepts. The idea of "white males managing adults" being superior to "women taking care of children and curricular issues" being superior to "minorities supervising other minorities" is a decades-old educational tradition (Yeakey et al., 1986). Because of legislation and other pressures to change, many past overt barriers are now reappearing in more subtle guises. For women to make personal strides forward, breaking glass ceilings, climbing old walls, and dumping the baggage of the past takes concerted effort. Such powerful effort commands concentrated attention, planning, and cohesiveness. The synergy of many forces is creating possibilities for a different future. Let us look at those possibilities in the next chapter.

2

Seizing the Catalysts of Today

Several contemporary phenomena are synergistically creating new possibilities for the leadership advancement of women. A critical combination of six factors creates an environment conducive to women's obtaining administrative positions:

- Administrative demographics
- Messiahs, scapegoats, and sacrificial lambs
- Extended visions of possibilities
- Expanding roles in schooling
- More comfortable graduate school settings
- Changed internal influences

Administrative Demographics

A quick look at administrative demographics signals impending vacancies in a range of leadership positions. Having been hired in massive numbers in the early 1960s to educate the baby boomers, present educational leaders are retiring or preparing to retire in massive numbers. More than half of today's high-ranking educational leaders, in their late 50s or early 60s, have adequate years of service in state systems to retire.

Fiscal policies attempting to offset the high salaries of veteran administrators result in job vacancies. To encourage more immediate openings in the highest paid ranks, some states have reduced maximum retirement benefits to 25 years of service rather than 30 years. For instance, the State of Illinois, in cooperation with local districts, will purchase 5 years of service for veterans who retire 5 years early. This program has encouraged shifts throughout the ranks.

Turnovers, for whatever reason, begin a domino effect of vacancies in other positions and districts. As an example, consider what often occurs when a system hires a new superintendent. A buyout package may be initiated as an incentive to remove the old guard to bring in new staff. A superintendent's retirement or move to a different school system sparks a catalyst that motivates others to change systems or retire early at several administrative levels, possibly influencing fluctuation in several school districts.

Retirement possibilities coincide with increases in school enrollments, estimated at 15%. These increases in the size of the student body at all levels of schooling caused *Working Woman* magazine, in an article entitled "The 25 Hottest Careers," (1993) to cite educational leadership as a field holding tremendous opportunity for women. The article estimates that, nationally, 62,000 educational administrators will be needed within the next few years. Entry-level salaries range from $45,000 to $52,000 with top-level salaries from $55,000 to $90,000.

Opportunities related to educational demographics are paralleled in other arenas. Traditionally, the biggest barrier to a woman's gaining political office has been the male incumbent. Retirement, death, and, occasionally, criminal indictment are opening long-entrenched political avenues for women (Roberts, 1992).

Other signs that cracks are appearing in the male leadership establishment are apparent in public attitude toward women in leadership roles as identified in political surveys. In 1984, only 28% of the population felt that the country would be better if more women held office. By 1992, support for women holding political office rose to 61% (Roberts, 1992). And another traditional male bastion, the American Medical Association, reports that between 1972 and 1992 the percentage of women graduating from medical schools grew from 8.9% to 38.2%.

In school districts in recent years, more women have gathered experience as principals, and others have added district office experience. Larger numbers of women have completed graduate programs in educational leadership, also strengthening their qualifications for promotions. When increased experience as middle managers and stronger credentials are added to opportunities provided by large numbers of vacancies as well as the growing public support for women in leadership roles, women become viable candidates for key positions. Such positive combinations intensify the possibilities and probabilities that women will assume important leadership roles.

These combinations were confirmed in a follow-up study, sponsored by the American Association of School Administrators, of a group of 75 women who had received administrative training. Jones and Montenegro (1982) located patterns that assisted or prohibited women's career advancement. They found that the women who had a strong collection of job experiences, initially presented in clearly designed résumés and accompanied by strong letters of reference, had made significant career advancement. Combinations prohibiting advancement interlinked lack of mobility, limited attempts to apply for jobs, and failure to consider one's life goals.

As larger numbers of women become skilled and knowledgeable about the behaviors needed to attain key leadership positions, women will be found in progressively higher ranks. This steady increase brings us closer to a critical mass where the percentage of women in decision-making positions will be self-sustaining.

Messiahs, Scapegoats, and Sacrificial Lambs

Roles as messiahs, scapegoats, and sacrificial lambs provide some career openings and promotions for women in educational administration. Default situations are often offered to women. Many school boards, commonly in inner cities, face school leadership and even district leadership where a number of men have failed as leaders. With their backs to a wall, hiring a woman is the only remaining choice. This situation is especially common in the too rare instances when minority women are given administrative positions.

As Yeakey et al. (1986) summarized, African American women, already in a double bind, are often presented with the chance to be "messiahs or scapegoats." They are awarded "minority schools" that have been poorly maintained and badly managed. These schools have been staffed with "pass-the-turkey" candidates unacceptable in schools with more vocal, politically active, and demanding principals and parents. Because of continuous openings from double or triple the turnover rate of other schools, these schools are also heavily staffed with beginning teachers. The critical nature of a physical facility and climate on the constant verge of emergency prohibits the proper attention, support, and guidance to beginning staff. After a few months of trial by fire, many young teachers exit the profession.

The irony of this dismal picture is that in such an environment, many women have proven to be messiahs. Bringing the first glimpses of care and commitment complemented by a different leadership style, many of these women have been highly successful. Carol Beck, principal of Thomas Jefferson High School in Brooklyn, New York, models the messiah. In a school reeling from the nearly daily loss of students to violent death, Ms. Beck has challenged the community and supported the emotional needs of her students and staff. Through her work with the community, her school has become a safe haven in the war zone of their community (Flax, 1992).

In interviews with exemplary women leaders, a recurring theme surrounding their first chances at administrative positions involved being offered "a special challenge." Routinely, women have been given the news that they are receiving an administrative position with a caveat attached. The caveat usually involves or involved going in to clean up a mess of some type. Messes can include combinations of accreditation failures, financial disasters, lack of community support, low morale among staff members, poor academic performance, and various other consequences of poor leadership. These first administrative assignments often come at any time during the school year after a disaster has occurred, such as a tragic death, when a previously unscrupulous principal finally became accountable, or in the middle of any scandal.

Commonly, messes stem from incompetent staff members whom no one bothered to document for dismissal. One supervisor in her first principalship recalled being assigned a teacher who sometimes just did not show up and, often, when he did arrive, was dirty and bloodied from hunting all night. Once she even found him cleaning his game in the classroom with students wandering about. Careful documentation with consistent observation by the principal created an atmosphere uncomfortable enough that the teacher resigned in 3 months.

Another principal was told to "take names and kick butt" as she entered a long-neglected middle school. She followed a series of four variously incompetent, chemically dependent, or retired-in-place principals. Much of the staff reflected past personnel shortcomings. During the first year, the principal recalled requiring that a physical education instructor wear underwear under his gym shorts; encouraging 11 faculty members to enter alcohol and drug treatment programs; relocating a secretary who informed teachers about the principal's location, observation schedule, telephone calls, and visitors; spearheading a major facilities repair and cleanup; and pressuring other staff to resign or retire. By the second year, a new culture permeated the school with rejuvenated staff, some new faces, and renewed pride by the entire school community in the facility and academic expectation.

Unfortunately, "sacrificial lamb" may also be added to administrative options of messiah or scapegoat. After successfully fighting major battles, many of the women interviewed were considered too controversial for promotions. Some even experienced the loss of their positions when problems were conquered. One inner-city assistant principal recalled being demoted from a principalship in another high school after making tough personnel decisions, requiring that the cafeteria not operate with a deficit balance, and enforcing other district policies that had long been ignored. The changes she made were essential but disturbed the culture enough to cost her the principalship. Tackling injustices and attaining major renovation necessarily ruffles the status quo and is often a thankless position, except for the personal satisfaction of knowing that good decisions were implemented for children and learning.

Regardless of how the positions finally come their way, women have often metaphorically taken lemons and produced lemonade. They have gained valuable experience and impressed others with the competence of women effectively handling crises or critical administrative roles. Many of the women interviewed recalled the growth that came from such experiences. Achieving the seemingly impossible gave women the chance to learn new skills, extend their visibility, gain job advancement, and make positive contributions. One woman recalled receiving a promotion in another system because the job she had previously accomplished demonstrated her ability to successfully "do things differently."

Extended Visions of Possibilities

Extended visions of possibilities are established as more women move to the forefront of district, state, and national leadership. As it becomes more customary to see women in leadership positions and as they assume new roles, other women in the wings are observing and establishing extended visions of possibility.

With women becoming entrenched in decision-making positions, second and third ripples of opportunities are provided for other women. As more women serve as principals, they place competent female teachers into essential roles, guiding them within collaborative settings. Dopp and Sloan's 1986 study of women in superintendencies found that they routinely encourage and recruit women and minority entry into educational leadership positions. As superintendents, they not only continue to mark the path necessary for moving forward but share a commitment to help others imagine and begin their own paths. Leadership shortages and the critical need for excellence in all schools underscore the importance of fostering leadership potential.

Expanding Leadership Dimensions in Schooling

Definitions of leadership tasks have expanded. A range of new dimensions and responsibilities has been added to schools, providing new opportunities for leadership. Consequently, people with new skills and insights are needed to successfully meet such responsibilities. Expanded definitions of what schools are all about create a need for different administrative positions requiring unique skill combinations (Hill, 1994a).

Many of the emerging positions are concentrated in school district offices. In some cases, new positions are being established. But in others, revamped job descriptions embody familiar job titles. School district offices have been affected by as much change as any other area of schooling. Buzz phrases such as "new century visions," "restructuring," "reform movements," and "site-based decision making" press district offices to reexamine the way they do business. Rather than focusing on inspection, job dimensions are reshaped to provide service, support, and guidance.

Gaining skills and positioning one's self in any of the following four areas would seem to pay off in placement in an administrative position in a short time.

Technology Supervisor. Due to the avalanche of technological change, principals, superintendents, and other administrators no longer can stay current regarding the information they need to purchase technology, much less to provide faculty and staff development. Technology supervisors are emerging leaders in schools and school districts. Their expert power and significant budget responsibility establish this as a key administrative position, in many cases, at the assistant superintendent level.

Technology supervisors are needed to help teachers restructure curricular approaches and design different ways of working with units of students. Planning for technology purchasing, staff and faculty development, interdistrict and intradistrict communication networks, and district problem solving make this position essential to the viability, survival, and advancement of any school district.

Agency Liaison for Integrated Services. Agency liaisons can help better serve children and their families while more effectively using tax dollars. They coordinate services and support for children and families from referral through follow-up stages. Along with health and counseling assistance, such services improve school attendance for a large segment of students who need optimal school opportunities to succeed.

Agency liaisons demonstrate tact, keen interpersonal skills, and creative problem solving to connect resources with programs. Refined and subtle interpersonal skills are required to deftly merge turf issues into the best service program possible. Clearer communications between agencies, schools, and families lead to greater effectiveness and trust throughout wide circles in the community.

Human Resources Director. Personnel methods practiced in the past are being replaced by much more sophisticated philosophies regarding the value of employees. Human resource directors in school districts are designing competency-based hiring processes seeking self-actualized, hardy personnel. Comprehensive attitudinal surveys and aptitude instruments are becoming as commonplace for use in school districts as they are in corporate personnel offices. The crisis in health care demands development of wellness programs to address behavior detrimental to personal health. Ever more complicated legal issues affecting today's workplace also add constantly evolving dimensions to human resources.

Community Coordinator. Fortunately, most school districts are being bombarded with a hodgepodge of offers of help and support from volunteers and business. The huge task of schooling requires all the assistance possible, but someone needs to sort through, screen, and connect resources. Community coordinators design volunteer programs encompassing orientation, training, and recognition. They are necessarily policy developers, public relations analysts, and marketing experts.

These four emerging titles and related dimensions of long-familiar positions are continually redefining, expanding, and reshaping. Forward-thinking districts seek personnel with the flexibility and lifelong learning mentality to be equipped and ready to explore unknown territory.

More Comfortable
Graduate School Settings

Women are encountering more comfortable graduate school settings in educational leadership for two interlinked reasons: (a) Administrative preparation program approaches and content are "getting real" and (b) more women and minorities are becoming faculty members. Because of the mixture of these two factors, women students are finding curricula more compatible with their experiences and philosophies while simultaneously finding role models within easy proximity.

Recently, faculty positions have become possible for more women in educational leadership preparation institutions. Although they are still less likely to be tenured and are paid less, employment of women and those from minority groups is occurring for several reasons: (a) Existing faculty members in educational leadership are facing imminent retirement so that openings are available. (b) For moral and/or accreditation reasons, institutions are seriously seeking members of minority groups and women as faculty members. (c) Because women are enrolled in graduate programs in increasing numbers, female faculty members are needed to establish links and present more extensive models.

Throughout graduate programs, Yeakey et al. (1986) found a 20% increase in women doctoral candidates and a 338% increase in female enrollment in business courses. The portion of doctoral degrees conferred on women has moved from 28% in 1979 to 39% in 1994 and is expected to reach 45% by the year 2000 (Database, 1994). More specifically, a 1988 study by McCarthy, Kuh, Newell, and Iacona found that 60% of the students in educational leadership programs are women. Such facts are forcing changes in traditionally all-male departments and colleges.

For women who have been in these departments in recent years, changes are apparent. One former principal, now a member of an educational leadership department, recalls attending an educational leadership annual conference and being one of less than a dozen women in the 300 or so participants. Five years later, women make up nearly one third of the attendees, with women moving rapidly into positions of decision making in the organization.

In the early 1990s, one of the old guard was heard grumbling at the bar after the day's sessions at one professional conference. He was specifically angered about the audacity of women presenting at the conference. "What do these women know about what goes on in schools?" he fumed. The woman who overheard him simultaneously felt pity, anger, and amusement at his comment. He had last been an administrator in a public school in 1964. Every woman at the conference had been a school administrator at least 20 years more recently than he.

The Danforth Foundation, as well as other agencies and organizations, heavily influenced revising educational leadership preparation programs in the late 1980s. They also support the efforts of women new to faculty ranks. Through formal and informal means, women working with the 22 institutions involved with the Danforth Principal Preparation Network were provided insights and opportunities to learn the tenure and promotion game. This support came from Danforth Foundation activities and initiatives as well as from many of the male participants who willingly mentored women beginning the faculty phase of their careers. This was especially valuable where support and direction did not exist within their own institution. This segment of the male leadership of significant educational administrative programs and foundations recognized an untapped resource fresh from today's schools ready to battle rigid academic models.

One principal vividly recalls her aspirations to interview for a university faculty position after completing her doctoral degree at the same time that her husband completed his in the early 1980s.

With identical experience and degrees, they began searching for faculty positions. After forwarding applications and résumés to a job-clearing service provided by the American Association of Colleges of Teacher Education (AACTE), they drove to the AACTE national conference to see what job interviews would be waiting. Her husband had requests for interview appointments from five different universities. She received none. Ironically, times are changing and many educational leadership departments are now specifically seeking women faculty members.

In addition to adding female and minority representation in faculty ranks, small but significant numbers of educational leadership programs are reforming approaches to preparing school leaders. A recognition exists that within school leadership, the Lone Ranger is dead. Schools and school systems can no longer be led by benevolent dictators. For its survival, contemporary education requires leaders with new sets of skills. Many women are emerging from reformed preparation programs equipped with the essential skills and insights for redesigning school structures to meet the needs of families and children.

Graduate students fresh from or still in the "real world" of schools have long groaned at the lack of fit of traditional programs that were lecture dominated, rigid theory-bound models with limited scope applying to hypothetical schools serving Ozzie and Harriet families. Reformed programs are problem based, thematic, theory-tied-to-practice models. They teach skill development linked to field experiences through team teaching, simulation, and technology structures. Tight partnerships with school districts influence and form the degree program.

Residency requirements forcing doctoral students to leave their jobs were acceptable in the past for a privileged few. Rarely was this possible for women. Now, even women who are single parents can meet innovative residency plans at many institutions designed to expand their skills and horizons but not requiring them to give up their jobs. The blend of faculty with recent school experience and a variety of backgrounds coupled with educational leadership programs with flexibility and reality bases are becoming a symbiotic environment for women to grow and develop leadership potential.

Newly emerging graduates from these programs are suggesting that present models produced in antiquated programs of the past be recalled for repairs or sold for scrap.

Changed Internal Influences

Changed internal influences are apparent in younger women. A new generation of women are shedding baggage carried by their mothers. An example can be found in the political arena where younger female political candidates have their sights set on higher political office than did women of past generations. They exude more confidence about the probability of their success. They exhibit strategies that cause traditional campaign principles to be rewritten. Campaigning in hospitals or other locations with heavy numbers of female employees rather than the established male centers exemplifies the shift in thinking and strategy. Women's issues have also been given a new focus within platforms of both parties. Health care, sexual harassment, day care, and abortion capture headlines. Economic concerns are also more keenly mirrored in the ballot box when women, long struggling and increasingly going it alone, vote in high numbers.

Young women are also shedding sex role stereotypes that limit career aspirations. Female high school seniors reflect a more ambitious vision of the future. In 1992, 35% of high school female seniors planned to go to graduate school or attain professional degrees compared to 9% 20 years earlier (Lawton, 1994). *Attitudes and expectations are changing.* No longer do women just hold jobs, whereas men have careers.

Motherhood has been an essential role that some women can balance while continuing a career. Other women select to forego a career and enter an alternative path later. Just as in Kelly and Guy's 1991 study of public administrators, the reality does still exist that women "with heavy family obligations seldom reach managerial ranks" (p. 411). Without easily accessible day care and elderly adult care as well as other community supports in place, career choices and advancements can be limited for many women. Internal and societal barriers may restrain women at certain points in their lives yet may be overcome elsewhere along a career path.

Final Thoughts

Today's successful women in leadership roles in various fields are perplexing to many people. Most have not used stereotypes from the past. They disregard these stereotypes and reach positions of importance through competence and valid experiences. Proven success in the past has propelled them into significant positions of authority. Women have achieved leadership while still respecting and enjoying the company of men. They can also relish their roles as mothers and have other women as friends, mentors, and protégées.

Women in a variety of fields are changing paradigms and creating new visions of possibilities. Instead of trying to find jobs, women have been developing their own. Half of the American companies owned by women have been started since 1980 (Kosnett, 1992). Although, generally, these companies are small, they employ 11 million people and are developing into lean, stable organizations more able to ride the current of economic change that often can damage giant, slower moving industries.

Changes are also happening in countries traditionally offering severe sanctioning on female behavior. In India, for instance, changes can be seen from the results of a 1988 study of female job attitudes and opportunities in the information technology field. Saldanha found that the women in her study felt quite dedicated to their careers. They reported that their careers, more than just jobs, offered extensive personal satisfaction. Although these women still experienced restrictions on business travel, their successful career development demonstrates a massive cultural change from recent Indian mores.

Political redefinitions are also being created by women. Hillary Clinton has presented a dilemma for many people. She is perplexing because she is bright, pleasant, and capable of biting back with wit and a smile. Whether or not one agrees with her political views, her competence in designing a plan of action and carrying it out is obvious. Along her career path, she has earned more money than her husband without emasculating him. She has frustrated many opponents because she handles traditional roles of the presidential wife while simultaneously serving the country as a policymaker.

This disparity between generational views causes some discomfort. Middle-aged women are challenged to sculpt a new definition of self while facing the changes naturally evolving as one ages. They are forging this definition in a world not smoothly blended between a variety of ranges of societal expectations and mores about women.

This dynamic is equally uncomfortable to many men who are supportive of women and aware of past disparity. Often, fathering a daughter has provided new awareness and perspectives for men who had never considered the barriers to women along career paths. Men comfortable with their personal image of self are comfortable, understanding, and respectful of women's new dimensions.

In educational settings, this evolution means that younger teachers have different concepts of their professional role. They will expect to be part of the decision-making, political, budgetary process within their schools. Understandings of the broader relationship and newly expanded definition of the mission of schools will be easier to assimilate. If young teachers decide to leave classroom environments, middle-management positions with clerical overtones will not be the limit of their sites. Their strength, wider experiences, self-confidence, and awareness will shatter glass ceilings.

3

Envisioning the Future

Predicting the future by reading a crystal ball is accomplished only in fiction. Prediction of success by reading a metaphorical crystal ball is easier when one has experienced success—obviously. This chapter focuses on the women interviewees' response to the question, "What trends do you perceive for women in public school administration?" This question was posed not necessarily to elicit their interpretations of the literature—of any particular published reports—but more to gather their perceptions, *based on their experiences*, of trends. As a basis for comparison and reflection, the literature is examined and summarized as appropriate.

The overwhelming tenor of the responses is positive. In general, the trends predicted include visions of more opportunities for women in a greater variety of areas and at earlier points in their careers. Therefore, the interviewees predict more successes for women in administrative positions in the very near future.

Predictions

One high school principal believes that, in the past, many men moved into administration to get out of the classroom. Often, these men never really wanted to be in the classroom; many were coaches who never entered the field to specialize in teaching. After some years of successful coaching, they were "rewarded" with administrative positions in their districts. This trend is diminishing, she feels, due largely to increasing calls for performance evaluation of both teachers and administrators. To conduct evaluations of teachers, one must understand and be trained in observation and supervision of good teaching. These skills are very different from the skills used by many coaches. Districts are therefore more careful in selecting good teachers, not necessarily good coaches, for administrative positions. Because the teaching ranks are populated largely by women, it follows that more women than men can demonstrate excellence as teachers to later be given opportunities for assistant principal and principal positions. As women demonstrate competence and collegiality in those roles, they are moved into higher positions with greater influence over more teachers and administrators.

To measure competence, in most states, principals are evaluated through scheduled as well as unscheduled observations. The first observation is preceded by a meeting with the evaluator during which time the principal states her or his goals for the year. Generally, postobservation conferences are held after any scheduled or unscheduled observations, with debriefing of the evaluation process. Sometimes the annual goals are solely the principal's; sometimes the evaluator adds or changes goals to better meet her or his perceptions of school and district needs. In any event, several major categories compose the criteria by which the principal is evaluated. Leadership, management, interpersonal skills, and demonstration of professionalism are common themes.

Similar evaluations occur for central office administrators. In larger districts, several assistant superintendents and/or directors of programs are involved with personnel, curriculum, finance, athletics, and special education. Usually, categories for evaluation of superintendents are similar to those for principals. When these sorts of evaluations are used, women have chances to demonstrate measurable competencies equal to men's chances.

In a different focus, one interviewee, an elementary school principal, explained that, in her opinion, women are proving to be more organized and harder workers than most men. Women have managed households, including budgets, while also doing a good job of teaching, a position that also requires multiple levels of skill in managing a multiplicity of tasks and personalities. In addition, she points out that women do especially well in balancing budgets in reduced funding times.

The perceptions of this interviewee are supported in the literature in various ways. Hammond and Fong (1988) found that women who demonstrated the highest levels of physical well-being and lowest levels of depression in her study occupy multiple roles: wife, mother, and paid worker, when compared with women who occupy fewer roles. Career satisfaction, in the Hammond and Fong study, was significantly predicted by personality traits called "hardiness" as well as "social support from friends" (p. 22).

Faye Crosby, in her book *Juggling: The Unexpected Advantages of Balancing Career and Home for Women and Their Families* (1991) comes to similar conclusions. She states that

> women who combine significant life roles are better off emotionally than are women with fewer roles. Even as they acknowledge stress and time pressure, jugglers demonstrate less depression, higher self-esteem, and greater satisfaction with life generally and with different aspects of life than do women who play fewer roles. There is also some indication that juggling enhances physical as well as psychological health. (p. 15)

In a later study, Newman (1993) found that women in higher education administration experience similar situations in occupying multiple roles. Furthermore, money was not the primary impetus for these women administrators. Rather, reasons for moving up the ranks revolved around desires to achieve autonomy and to make a difference in their field. They sought the responsibility of administrative roles, enjoying the diversity and other activities associated with being in charge.

A superintendent who was interviewed predicts that more and more women will aspire to positions as educational leaders, including the secondary principalship. She has already seen enough women moving into elementary principalships to say that that is not a prediction but a trend already in place. However, not enough women are going into nontraditional central office positions such as finance, but she feels that may change, too. In addition, she believes that more women in higher education positions will have a positive effect on women in graduate schools who aspire to administrative positions. She predicts that another 3 years will see *great* differences in the acceptance and recruitment of women into public school administration.

A 1992 College Board survey ("Report Reveals Decline," 1994) of full-time students enrolled for the fall of 1992 revealed that women outnumber men at colleges. Enrollment of women was 54% of the total student population at that time. The growing number of women in higher education administrative positions is further good news. Newman (1993) reports that in 1975 and 1980, women represented only 8.5% of all higher education administrative positions. In 1990, that number had grown to 38%. Furthermore, the U.S. Department of Education (1992) reports that the percentage of women principals (public and private schools combined) grew from 21.45% in the 1984-1985 school year to 30.0% in the 1990-1991 school year.

Another superintendent also predicts larger numbers of women in public school administration, particularly in principalships and superintendencies. She feels that more women in those roles will have the effect of better balancing the curriculum—less emphasis on athletics and more emphasis on the fine arts as equal in value. In addition, she sees a trend of more parent volunteers, both male and female. More volunteers will be needed in response to the push for greater parent involvement in schools generally but also essential as support staff in pinched budget times. In other words, she sees women administrators as promoting more balance and being more in tune with preparing students for life beyond the big Friday night game.

Interestingly, the House and Senate, as of August 1994, have approved versions of the Athletic Equity Disclosure Act (see "Bill Would Require," 1994). This bill would require higher education institutions to collect and release data on expenditures for women's and men's intercollegiate sports. Although this bill does not affect the fine arts, it does provide a measure of accountability in regard to gender issues. Perhaps the big Friday night game played by women athletes will eventually be funded to the same level as the men's games.

A political move that will have a greater effect in general on women's issues is that 33% of President Clinton's nominations to the federal bench (lifetime appointments) are women, compared to 6% for President Bush, 4% for President Reagan, and 3% for President Carter (News Quotes, 1994).

One interviewee predicted that more women will move into administration because people in general are now much more open to women as leaders. The qualities that women leaders (those whom she knows) demonstrate include business orientation plus intuitive skills. She states that the need for both qualities is now widely accepted in business and in education. This is in contrast to the outdated style of man-as-tough-leader image. Women, she claims, are more apt to be skilled in multifaceted ways and are less domineering in their leadership styles.

Anita Taylor (1984), in a speech to a conference of women researchers in Kentucky, made similar statements about the multifaceted skills that women bring to leadership positions. In particular, she refers to the current "information society." Women were at a distinct disadvantage in the days when physical strength was a key leadership skill. In the information age, however, lack of brawn is no disadvantage. Communication of information is a skill in which women can and do excel. Communication is much more important for leadership in public schools today than is brawn.

In 1985, Marshall found that the main tasks necessary for success in school administrative positions include (a) the ability to set goals and subgoals, (b) coordinated long-term goals and action plans, (c) the foresight to anticipate problems and assertively prepare solutions, and (d) the ability to effectively train others and delegate tasks. Not once is brawn mentioned! Faye Crosby (1991) makes a conclusion to the effect that being the cook, maid, chauffeur, and secretary may not be as much fun for many women as *hiring* the cook, maid, chauffeur, and secretary.

The expanding volume of feminist literature is predicted to be very influential by one interviewee, particularly the research about women's caring and communicative leadership styles. In other words, there is a growing body of research that "proves" that women are capable leaders.

The growing acceptance of women as leaders is evidenced in the increasing numbers of conferences focusing on the trend. 1994 sees the 10th Annual Women as Leaders Seminar in Washington, D.C. The American Council on Education supports the National Identification Program for Women in Higher Education Administration. Many states have leadership academies for women in public school administration. In addition, the Association of Teacher Educators supports a Commission on Gender Equity in Education, and the American Association of Colleges of Teacher Education supports the Committee on Women's Issues.

Another interviewee sees that the various directions in the overall school reform trend stress school, family, and community links requiring team building and site-based management—all necessitating skills and working relationships that seem to come naturally to women. Women, contrary to most men, in her observations, are able to make connections in the nonlinear ways required for these reform efforts. In addition, she feels that women are not threatened by empowering others; rather, they are more adept at empowering and team building than are men.

Potential Downsides

One interviewee pointed out that there is a need to hire more men for teaching positions but fewer men are available in her district. In addition, currently, the pool of women leaders is drained. Unless more recruitment is done for both areas, she sees few chances for women in administrative positions. This fear is echoed by another interviewee who states that the few women in administration in her state are so highly visible that if even one is less effective, she hurts them all.

Another interviewee predicts a resurgence of male egos in administration as the economy tightens and men change careers into education. In particular, the programs for moving former military men into education will fuel this trend. She concluded, however, that this will heighten the quality of competition for both men and women and thus will probably be a good thing.

In summary, the predictions made by the women interviewees are their perceptions of trends. These perceptions are based on their backgrounds, their recent experiences, and their varying degrees of facility in "crystal ball gazing."

Health Issues

As more and more women move into leadership roles, not only in public schools but in the business world, more pressure is being put on researchers to look at issues of health for women. The picture on medical research for women is changing for the 1990s and, predictably, beyond. Although the outdated attitude that women's health is different from men's health only once a month is still too common, according to Andrew Grogan (1993), that attitude is changing.

In 1987, 13.5% of the National Institute of Health's $6 billion research budget was devoted to diseases unique to or more serious for women. For the 1990s, the Women's Health Initiative is a multimillion dollar federal research endeavor that will provide data on various women's health issues. In addition, the Office of Women's Health was established in 1990 by the National Institute of Health. This office will seek to involve 70,000 women in research on postmenopausal health concerns, including cardiovascular disease, osteoporosis, and breast and uterine cancers.

It is also encouraging to note growing numbers of women practitioners in various medical fields. According to Aburdene and Naisbitt (1992), at least 50% of new primary care physicians in the United States are women. Furthermore, half the resident medical students in obstetrics and gynecology today are women.

Menopause, according to some, could easily become *the* health issue of the 1990s and beyond. Menopause has commonly been thought to cause depression associated with the loss of the ability to bear children. However, Aburdene and Naisbitt (1992), in *Megatrends for Women*, report on a 5-year study of 2,500 women that indicated that three fourths of the women felt either relieved or neutral, rather than negative, about menopause. Only 3% of the interview group considered menopause a negative thing. Those statistics are borne out by the majority of women interviewed for this book. Many of the interviewees report the most satisfying times of their lives as being in the leadership roles that they have attained in post-childbearing years. (See Chapter 8 for more data.)

PART II

Strategies for Professional and Self-Development

The first step toward upward mobility involves analyzing personal and professional goals, competencies, and potential. A woman who thinks she wants an administrative position in public schools today must be proactive. In so doing, she must be aware of long-standing discriminatory policies and be willing to find paths around those obstacles. Previous chapters examine many of these obstacles as interactive, involving both societal and organizational levels. Part II contains concrete methods for analyzing and assessing individual competencies as well as gut-level advice from successful women administrators about making or finding paths.

One of the reasons women seek administrative positions is to increase earnings. Although, historically, men have received higher pay for equal titles, the wage gap is narrowing. One of the reasons for the gap has been the discontinuity in years of work that many women have had due to taking time out for children and traditional wife roles (Miller-Loessi, 1992, p. 4). That "traditional" role is being redefined in the 1990s. Another reason for wage gaps has been occupational segregation by gender. In public school administration, there is a danger of this phenomenon continuing if women dominate principalships only in elementary schools, for example. However, as more women obtain secondary principalships and central office roles in finance and the superintendency, gender integration will occur and wage disparity will be a thing of the past. This process has been dubbed "the trickle-up effect" by Nannerl Keohane (1991).

In gathering data to support the general optimistic stance of women in leadership roles in public school and in North American workplaces in general, the following list of legislation, events, and publications is encouraging (Sandler, 1994).

Highlights of Legislation, Events, Publications Important to Women Leaders

1964 Title VII of the Civil Rights Act includes prohibitions of discrimination in employment on the basis of gender.

1972 Title IX is enacted to prohibit discrimination on the basis of gender in federally assisted education programs.

1970s Workplace cases eventually result in courts' determining that sexual harassment is gender discrimination.

1979 The first report on campus sexual harassment of students is published (Bernice Sandler at the Project on the Status and Education of Women).

1980 The U.S. Equal Employment Opportunity Commission (EEOC) issues sexual harassment guidelines for employers, quid pro quo, and hostile environment.

1980-1981 The first study on peer sexual harassment in high schools is conducted (Nan Stein for the Massachusetts Department of Education).

1985 A guideline for teenagers concerning sexual harassment is published (University of Michigan; "Tune Into Your Rights," 1985).

1989 The first state law is passed that requires every school in the state to develop and post a policy on sexual harassment, including consequences for violating the policy.

1991 The Civil Rights Act of 1991 is enacted, allowing employees to recover damages from an employer.

1992 The AAUW Report *How Schools Shortchange Girls* is published.

1993 The Hill-Thomas hearings legitimize sexual harassment as an issue.

1993 The U.S. Supreme Court rules unanimously that a person who claims sexual harassment in the workplace need not prove that she or he was psychologically damaged or unable to do her or his job because of sexual harassment (*Harris v. Forklift Systems*).

1993 *Failing at Fairness: How America's Schools Cheat Girls* by Myra and David Sadker is published.

1993 *Hostile Hallways: The AAUW Survey on Sexual Harassment in America's Schools* is published.

1993 The Gender Equity in Education Act includes programs to provide teachers with skills to remove gender bias from the classroom.

More formal networking of women in politically active roles may be necessary before large-scale gender integration occurs in some demographic areas. More reactive situations, such as litigation to redress gender bias, may be necessary in some instances. The primary focus of Part II, however, is on proactive issues.

A Sample Process
for Breaking the Glass Ceiling

- Discussion of goals with an administrative colleague
- Consultation with university faculty in educational administration department
- Demographic data gathering
- Planned mobility
- Paper-pen critical analysis of skills, attitudes, energy level
- Development of a strategic plan

4

Developing and Assessing
Our Leadership Competency

One's first teaching assignment, as anyone's first job, heavily influences one's perceptions about work cultures. Teaching is the professional entry-level position for nearly every educational leader. Contrary to some assumptions about leadership, many educational leaders stay in the classroom. Others move to principalships, university faculty positions, superintendencies, district office positions, or along a variety of agency, governmental, and entrepreneurial avenues.

To become leaders as roles are explored during a 20- to 40-year career, educators have to adjust or bury many early assumptions about work cultures. Generations of teachers become accustomed to roles of isolation and treatment as subservient employees. With the exception of initiatives in some perceptive school districts supporting collaboration, teachers are conditioned not to discuss their practice. Even less probable are possibilities for teachers to consider, or even be consulted regarding, essential decisions about school functions such as allocation of school budgets to better serve students. In situations where teachers are still treated so menially and the sacred station of textbooks and workbooks still exists, administrators seek textbooks that are "teacher proof." In classroom cell after classroom cell, secluded teachers still reinvent the wheel, attempting to discover how to best meet the needs of students.

Similarly, administrators in the recent past did not regard themselves as leaders because they also carried managerial baggage from the examples modeled for them. A principal thought he or she must dominate the faculty to be successful. Teachers were kept in the dark regarding the way the system worked, the amount and use of the budget, and the routes available to gather information or accomplish goals. Faculty meetings, a great misnomer, were used as a platform for principals to talk to teachers. Schedules were made for teachers. Supplies were ordered for teachers. With everything being done *for* and *to* teachers, power was retained in the principal's office.

This hierarchical relationship of the all-powerful principal and subservient teachers fits other employer/employee models of the time when secretaries made coffee and picked up the boss's dry cleaning. This model also certainly mimicked acceptable male/female roles. Principals regarded themselves as benevolent dictators taking care of their sheep. One district director recalls the anger she felt as a teacher in learning that her former principal casually referred to the faculty as his "harem."

Many women who achieved early administrative roles did so by mimicking the hierarchical model. They often struggled with balancing the demands of their supervisors with the discomfort of working with teachers in this way. To guard against criticism for putting a woman into a principalship, superintendents had to be vigilant for signs of weakness. Early women school leaders, as pathfinders, were held in close scrutiny from all directions.

In the past, women who pioneered leadership in many fields were advised to imitate male strategies. "But the old ways didn't work for anyone, and no one knew how to manage under the new circumstances. That freed up the most creative people to start experimenting" (Aburdene & Naisbitt, 1992, p. 88). The era of the hierarchical structure as an acceptable, much less functional, model for schooling and most other organizational structures has ended. Changes in philosophy about effective leadership has created new terminology. In enlightened schools, administrators no longer consider how to *handle* teachers but instead find ways to *empower*. Decision making within the educational setting is not *directive* but rather *collaborative*.

New Influences on Concepts of Leadership

Two influences are at work changing or redefining our concepts of leadership. First, a wider population is envisioned as having leadership potential. Early research in the area of leadership was conducted by white men about white men. Consideration of a population including women and minorities brings new dimensions to the concept of leadership. After years of hiding such competencies, women are now willing to call on their abilities to foster and influence the growth of others in the organization. Hagberg (1984) discusses the advantage that women have in being "naturally socialized" with skills complementing the leadership maturity necessary to move to the enlightened power stage. Managers begin with an emphasis on the raw power stage, exemplified by time spent seeking larger desks, bigger offices, longer titles, better views. Experienced, mature managers move to the enlightened power stage as coaches for others.

The second influence creating an evolution in our concepts of leadership stems from organizational trends that include flattening traditional bureaucratic structures and decentralizing decision making. Images of leadership and organizations are being reshaped. Rather than top-down line and staff organizational charts common in the past, circular and flattened pancake symbols are now used to visualize new structures. "If empowerment is the first attribute of women's leadership, creating the organization structure to foster it is the second" (Aburdene & Naisbitt, 1992, p. 95).

Studies of women managers have confirmed their ability to be less conventional in problem solving and more at ease with creative innovation. Women comfortably adapt to flexible, evolving struc-

TABLE 4.1 Dimensions of Emerging Leadership Skills

Desired Skills	As Opposed To
Information collection	The Lone Ranger
Problem analysis	All knowing
Interpersonal sensitivity	Iron fist
Motivating others	"This is a mandatory in-service."
Public relations	Isolated kingdoms

tures of organizations (Feuer, 1988). Characteristics of leaders for contemporary educational settings have shifted from 1950s, 1960s, 1970s, or 1980s models. The new century truly brings a changed focus.

Emerging skills of leadership mean that new terminology is being created and discussed (see Table 4.1). For instance, "tolerance for ambiguity" is a desired quality. Such consideration of "gray areas" would have been unheard of just a few years ago in the black-and-white world of management. DePree (1992) discusses the misconception "that a manager is either in control or not in control" (p. 11). Rather, he identifies the practice of equity as essential. Equity includes providing fair distribution of resources and further considers human relationships. In her monograph, Weller (1988) outlines skills required of contemporary leaders. She identifies "softer" skills, such as showing consideration of people and cooperative leadership, as well as "harder" skills, such as developing strategies for building a base of power.

The National Policy Board for Educational Administration (Thomson, 1993) used a gender and ethnically mixed sampling of administrators to develop 21 skill and knowledge areas needed for the principalship. Traditional lists of administrative skills abound, appraising leadership, judgment, oral and written skills, and legal and regulatory applications. Different twists are evident in the 1992 assessment. These changes are dramatic.

Changes in the concept of leadership are evident not only in studies of the school principalship but are obvious in business and other professions. This changing emphasis appears in Hammons and Keller's 1990 study of competencies desired in community col-

lege presidents. Skill components involving interpersonal relationships, information processing, network building, imparting a
vision, and delegation were part of the leadership dimensions identified as essential by surveyed higher education administrators.
When personal characteristics were rated, a sense of humor, emotional balance, risk taking, wellness, positive attitude, flexibility,
creativity, empathy, and patience were added to traditional aspects,
such as judgment, sense of responsibility, integrity, and communication.

To explore perceptions concerning their leadership skills,
women in our interviews were asked to list five words that others
would use to describe their leadership style. When characteristics
are divided into synonymous clusters, study participants predominantly felt that they are viewed as problem solvers and creators of
vision and ideas. The second most common group of identifiers indicate that they hold and demonstrate high expectations of performance for themselves and others. The third area most heavily
reported involved their concern with representing trustworthiness,
fairness, dependability, and honesty in dealing with people.

Although departing from traditional definitions, an analysis of
their lists naturally jelled around the two dimensions cited in educational leadership literature from the Ohio State Studies (Lunenburg
& Ornstein, 1991): initiating structure and consideration. Table 4.2
represents categories into which the words of our study's participants' could be classified. Samples of exact terms selected can be
found within each category.

Categorizing Traps

When broader definitions of school leadership are narrowed to
studies of instructional leadership, gender differences are found.
Women spend more time on the curricular and instructional aspect
of the principalship and are more likely to be perceived by their staff
as exemplifying instructional leadership than are men (Andrews &
Basom, 1990). Generally, female principals in Andrews and Basom's
(1990) studies have taught for longer periods before becoming principals and have stronger curricular backgrounds. Andrews and

TABLE 4.2 Women Leaders' Descriptors of How Others Would Describe Their Leadership Style

Percentage	Number	Category and Sample Terms
Initiating structures		
23	35	Creative problem solvers and developers of vision and ideas
		Sample terms: innovative, visionary, sees broad dimensions, lifelong learner
18	27	Demanding of self and others
		Sample terms: assertive, perfectionist, task oriented, productive, rolls up sleeves, committed, driven, confident
6.5	10	Competent manager
		Sample terms: organized, clear, practiced, thorough
Consideration		
16	24	Models integrity
		Sample terms: honest, dependable, trustworthy, candid, direct, fair
9	14	Involves others
		Sample terms: participatory, empowering, facilitator, delegator, collaborative, team builder, inclusive
8.5	13	Approachable
		Sample terms: listener, compassionate, considerate, down home, open, helpful
6.5	10	Motivational
		Sample terms: enthused, encourager, positive
6.5	10	Supportive
		Sample terms: sensitive, appreciative, understanding, respectful, coaching
6	9	Disposition
		Sample terms: patient, harmonious, low key, sense of humor, happy, humanistic, flexible

Basom also found that women elementary principals exhibited a greater concern for individual and developmental differences, communicated more positively, and conveyed the vision of the school more clearly than did men. Shakeshaft (1989) supported these findings and added that women use language that encourages community building, involve the community more often, and maintain a higher morale in schools. Women are also overrepresented in principalships in schools identified as highly successful.

However, when considering the characteristics and lists of competencies needed in an organizational leader, several writers have fallen into a detrimental trap by labeling competencies as male or female. By giving gender categories to these characteristics, we impede progress in finding the best leaders. *When we begin matching men and women to characteristics, we build socially acceptable boxes that mitigate and restrict the intricate and artistic blends of leadership qualities.* Over a decade ago, Naisbitt (qtd. in Zweig, 1983) characterized the changing and blending of gender roles as " 'a synthesis of the best qualities and characteristics of each, a reconciliation of what were once thought to be opposite values into a new whole' " (p. 138). Perhaps our need for leadership is so great that the optimum time has arrived for us to use our resources to develop the best and to select the best leaders regardless of gender descriptors.

Growing Through Self-Assessment

Self-assessment of leadership competencies allows one to identify areas of strength as well as the areas that need development. Three questions must be considered:

1. In what leadership areas am I particularly strong?
2. What areas need strengthening?
3. What strategies should be used to further develop my abilities?

Self-Assessment of Leadership Competencies

Self-assessment provides a starting point for examining skill development. A knowledge and skill base entitled *Principals for Our Changing Schools* (Thomson, 1993) was developed by widely representative practitioner groups sponsored by the National Policy Board for Educational Administration. See the appendix, beginning on page 55, for a self-assessment tool based on their conclusions.

Strategies to
Strengthen Leadership Skills

Many generic strategies exist for strengthening any areas you might identify for self-improvement. Consider the following suggestions:

- Read the literature on the specific area.
- Use reflective writing to analyze your growth and development in this skill area. Further outline where you want to go. Envision (a) how you will perform, (b) how you will benefit, and (c) how others will benefit when you have strengthened this area.
- Participate in a professional conference, workshop, or teleconference surrounding this topic.
- Identify people around you or people in national and/or international arenas who best exemplify excellence in this area. Read and study their approaches. If possible, contact and interview them about their personal growth and insights.
- Seek out a mentor and discuss your goals for development. Incorporate his or her suggestions into your plan.
- Offer this area as a topic for your network to explore. Collaborate on refinement and specific activities toward the goal. Your network can be close associates or expanded to an international audience through Internet or other information highways.

Now that you have a clearer picture of your talents and areas requiring an investment of time and energy, develop a time line to carry out the strategies you have outlined. Sequence some specific steps to be accomplished within the next 2 weeks. Gradually move to monthly objectives for the next year. Again, you will be more likely to follow through on this process if you jointly develop this plan with important members of your network or with a mentor. You may also want to use this as a professional development plan in your work setting after discussion with your supervisor.

Considering Hardiness

A final concept to consider in examining your career growth and development involves your hardiness. The basis for self-assessing hardiness stems from a theory grounded in a study beginning in 1977. Kobasa, Maddi, and other researchers at the University of Chicago conducted a study of several hundred middle- and upper-level managers employed by an Illinois public utility (cited in Pines, 1980). As would be expected in any group, they found that after a few years, middle managers had either advanced in the organization or remained stagnant.

More important findings highlighted a strong correlation between the stagnated group and higher incidences of stress-related illnesses (Kobasa, 1979; Kobasa, Maddi, & Courington, 1981). The stagnated group suffered from hypertension, back problems, higher incidences of heart disease, and other related health problems. In reviewing differences between the baseline profiles of these two groups, researchers found that the biggest differences involved personality factors that in the healthier group were subsequently designated as hardiness.

Hardiness Analysis

Hardy personalities are composed of three factors that interact to reduce debilitating effects of stress. They include the following:

Commitment. Employees with high levels of commitment to their organization or position feel that what they are doing is significant and important. Commitment increases individuals' ability to find meaning in the events in which they engage. Commitment is a big challenge facing women who are seeking educational administrative positions. Commitment has the power to overcome internal and external roadblocks established by sex role stereotyping.

Challenge or Change. Within the job and other life settings, change is greeted as inevitable and nonthreatening. Change is seen as challenging, stimulating, and an opportunity rather than a problem.

Internal Locus of Control. Employees who understand that they control direction and events and possess self-destiny within the organization have an internal locus of control. "Control enhances stress resistance perceptually by increasing the likelihood that events will be experienced as a natural outgrowth of one's actions" (Jarvis, 1992, p. 35).

The particular level of hardiness experienced at any given time within our jobs fluctuates due to innumerable factors. For instance, beginning educators may feel great commitment and respond well to change but feel no control because they lack experience and comparison to grasp the dynamics of the school. On the other hand, experienced educators have rolled with the pendulums of change and have found aspects of the job that they can control. After years of overflowing, underfunded classrooms and national reports emphasizing negative educational progress, the commitment level of beginning administrators can erode.

To assess our personal hardiness, we cannot concentrate only on today's impressions or mood. Rather, we need to recall our impressions over a longer time span of, at the very least, the past year. Reflect on the following:

COMMITMENT

1. Have you sensed feelings of joy or exhilaration about aspects of your job?

2. Have you felt a sense of pride when someone asked about what you do for a living?

3. Have you gained energy in the middle of a tiring day or project when you thought about the importance of the task?

4. Have you felt a desire to celebrate an accomplishment on your job?

5. Have you experienced a real satisfaction and peace of mind from a job-related accomplishment?

CHANGE

1. List five changes you have encountered on the job during the last year. Analyze each change in regard to the positive, negative, and ripple effects.

2. What risks have you considered taking on the job? Analyze the possible best and worst case scenarios.

CONTROL

1. List activities on the job for which you are completely responsible.

2. List times that your ideas, plans, or suggestions have been incorporated into the organization.

3. Consider how you personally have made a difference in your work setting.

Personal Hardiness Analysis

At this point, you are ready to compose a statement summarizing your impression of your personal hardiness.

A. Consider whether you most strongly feel:

1. Committed to your job

2. Able to respond positively to change

3. In control of your own destiny in your work setting

For each area, analyze the reasons for your strength.

B. Consider which of the three areas needs the most strengthening. Analyze why.

What behaviors or elements in your work setting need to change to strengthen this area?

C. Consider at what points during project development or during the academic or calendar year you experience the most hardiness.

D. Outline your personal goals to further develop your level of hardiness.

Summary

After self-assessing your leadership competencies and analyzing your hardiness, you have clarified skills and strengths. You have also formed some goals for your continued self-development. Putting these strategies into place requires reminders such as placing key activities toward strengthening a skill in your weekly or monthly calendar. After developing a clearer personal profile and after charting a path to achieve some professional goals, you can begin developing a broader view of factors that will assist you in attaining a position of leadership. The next chapters will supply other strategies for moving forward in school systems and other organizations.

APPENDIX

Self-Assessment of Leadership Competencies

Listed below are skills that leaders must be able to perform. Your task is to assess your experience with each skill. Read each skill statement and rate yourself according to the following scale. For example, how skilled are you at assuming responsibility when appropriate?

Circle 5 if you can perform the skill at an expert level.
Circle 4 if you can perform the skill with reasonable success.
Circle 3 if you have limited experience performing the skill.
Circle 2 if you have only seen others model the skill.
Circle 1 if you have no knowledge or had no opportunity to
        develop the skill.

In the column on the right, rate yourself by circling the appropriate number.

How skilled am I at the following:

LEADERSHIP
1. Assuming responsibility when appropriate   5 4 3 2 1
2. Analyzing negative and positive forces affecting my organization   5 4 3 2 1
3. Taking action when problems arise   5 4 3 2 1
4. Accepting authority when it is given   5 4 3 2 1
5. Setting priorities   5 4 3 2 1
6. Demonstrating a vision for the organization   5 4 3 2 1
7. Communicating and gathering support for the vision   5 4 3 2 1
8. Observing trends and recognizing implications   5 4 3 2 1
9. Modeling the core values of my organization   5 4 3 2 1

Sum the totals for each section and divide by the number of items to find section averages.   Average score
_____

INFORMATION COLLECTION
1. Gathering data and facts to make a decision   5 4 3 2 1
2. Knowing organizational rules and policy   5 4 3 2 1
3. Using a variety of sources to shape my organization's direction   5 4 3 2 1
4. Using technology to gather and make information accessible   5 4 3 2 1

Average score
_____

PROBLEM ANALYSIS
1. Demonstrating skills that assist people or groups to see more than one side of an issue   5 4 3 2 1
2. Knowing when to seek additional information   5 4 3 2 1
3. Identifying several alternatives in problem solving   5 4 3 2 1
4. Gathering input from all stakeholders   5 4 3 2 1

Average score
_____

JUDGMENT
1. Reaching logical, ethical, and bias-free conclusions   5 4 3 2 1
2. Making timely decisions   5 4 3 2 1
3. Giving priority to significant issues   5 4 3 2 1
4. Striving for equity in all decisions   5 4 3 2 1

Average score
_____

ORGANIZATIONAL OVERSIGHT
1. Planning my own work   5 4 3 2 1
2. Scheduling my time wisely   5 4 3 2 1
3. Establishing procedures to regulate activities   5 4 3 2 1

4. Helping others work more effectively   5 4 3 2 1
5. Meeting deadlines   5 4 3 2 1
6. Considering the "solution after next" (Nadler & Hibino, 1990)   5 4 3 2 1
7. Following through   5 4 3 2 1
8. Overseeing the development, implementation, and evaluation of long- and short-range goals   5 4 3 2 1
9. Ensuring that reward systems fit with goal attainment   5 4 3 2 1

Average score
_____

IMPLEMENTATION
1. Putting a plan into effect   5 4 3 2 1
2. Leading a group to task completion   5 4 3 2 1
3. Verifying progress along benchmarks toward a goal   5 4 3 2 1
4. Adjusting a plan that isn't working   5 4 3 2 1
5. Supporting personnel throughout work on a project   5 4 3 2 1

Average score
_____

DELEGATION
1. Identifying who can accomplish tasks   5 4 3 2 1
2. Checking on progress   5 4 3 2 1
3. Relinquishing authority with task responsibility   5 4 3 2 1
4. Providing opportunities for others to develop leadership skills   5 4 3 2 1
5. Supporting others as they develop their leadership skills   5 4 3 2 1
6. Ensuring that safety nets are in place in our organizational culture that foster risk taking   5 4 3 2 1

Average score
_____

INSTRUCTION AND THE LEARNING ENVIRONMENT
1. Understanding the developmental needs of the learner   5 4 3 2 1
2. Supporting a positive learning environment   5 4 3 2 1
3. Modeling a variety of strategies to support improved instruction   5 4 3 2 1
4. Supervising instruction   5 4 3 2 1
5. Establishing a school culture supportive of instructional excellence   5 4 3 2 1
6. Facilitating group analysis of a variety of learning and instructional assessments   5 4 3 2 1

Average score
_____

CURRICULUM DESIGN

1. Aligning curriculum with student outcomes   5 4 3 2 1
2. Implementing technology for support of curriculum   5 4 3 2 1
3. Conducting needs assessments to implement curricular change   5 4 3 2 1
4. Supporting staff planning and implementation of change in curriculum   5 4 3 2 1

Average score

_____

STUDENT GUIDANCE AND DEVELOPMENT

1. Providing for student guidance and counseling   5 4 3 2 1
2. Coordinating community agencies to meet needs of families   5 4 3 2 1
3. Planning for family and adult support programs   5 4 3 2 1
4. Coordinating a comprehensive program of student activities   5 4 3 2 1

Average score

_____

STAFF DEVELOPMENT

1. Identifying professional needs of staff   5 4 3 2 1
2. Facilitating programs to improve staff effectiveness   5 4 3 2 1
3. Providing specific feedback on performance   5 4 3 2 1
4. Fostering self-development of staff   5 4 3 2 1
5. Arranging for remedial help for staff in need   5 4 3 2 1
6. Involving staff in developing professional activities   5 4 3 2 1
7. Scheduling organizational time for reflection and personal goal setting   5 4 3 2 1

Average score

_____

MEASUREMENT AND EVALUATION

1. Identifying organizational needs   5 4 3 2 1
2. Analyzing staff needs   5 4 3 2 1
3. Installing measures to determine that outcomes meet or exceed standards or goals   5 4 3 2 1
4. Establishing relationships between curriculum, student outcomes, and varieties of assessment measures   5 4 3 2 1
5. Interpreting measures for others to understand   5 4 3 2 1
6. Designing a mechanism for accountability   5 4 3 2 1

Average score

_____

RESOURCE ALLOCATION

1. Planning and developing a budget	5 4 3 2 1
2. Procuring funds from a variety of sources	5 4 3 2 1
3. Evaluating the best use of resources to reach outcomes	5 4 3 2 1
4. Involving staff in budget design and determining priorities	5 4 3 2 1
5. Ensuring that budget allocation correlates with organizational priorities	5 4 3 2 1
6. Using technology and system approaches to expedite and manage budgetary processes	5 4 3 2 1
	Average score
	_____

MOTIVATING OTHERS

1. Creating conditions to enhance staff commitment	5 4 3 2 1
2. Establishing a participatory management focus	5 4 3 2 1
3. Recognizing effective performance	5 4 3 2 1
4. Coaching, guiding, giving feedback to staff	5 4 3 2 1
5. Serving as a role model irrespective of gender	5 4 3 2 1
6. Planning for celebration of accomplishments	5 4 3 2 1
7. Tying intrinsic and extrinsic rewards to performance and goal accomplishment	5 4 3 2 1
	Average score
	_____

INTERPERSONAL SENSITIVITY

1. Identifying the needs and concerns of others	5 4 3 2 1
2. Mediating conflict	5 4 3 2 1
3. Maintaining a physical and cultural environment considerate of others and the needs of the group	5 4 3 2 1
4. Recognizing cultural/ethnic differences	5 4 3 2 1
5. Displaying tact	5 4 3 2 1
6. Understanding differences in personal priorities	5 4 3 2 1
7. Recognizing achievements	5 4 3 2 1
	Average score
	_____

ORAL AND NONVERBAL EXPRESSION

1. Presenting information verbally	5 4 3 2 1
2. Adjusting content and delivery to the audience	5 4 3 2 1
3. Accepting and effectively giving feedback	5 4 3 2 1
4. Summarizing, clarifying, restating for the group	5 4 3 2 1
5. Avoiding cultural or gender-biased behaviors	5 4 3 2 1
	Average score
	_____

WRITTEN EXPRESSION
1. Expressing ideas clearly in writing   5 4 3 2 1
2. Adjusting content to the audience   5 4 3 2 1
3. Editing carefully   5 4 3 2 1
4. Using technology to expedite and refine writing   5 4 3 2 1
Average score
_____

PHILOSOPHICAL AND CULTURAL VALUES
1. Recognizing a variety of philosophical influences
   on the way schools operate   5 4 3 2 1
2. Reflecting an understanding of American culture   5 4 3 2 1
3. Demonstrating integrity at all times with all people   5 4 3 2 1
4. Identifying the complexity of views and diversity
   of values in a pluralistic culture   5 4 3 2 1
Average score
_____

LEGAL AND REGULATORY APPLICATIONS
1. Acting in accordance with standards, policies,
   and laws   5 4 3 2 1
2. Recognizing standards of liability   5 4 3 2 1
3. Understanding governing contract and account-
   ing policies   5 4 3 2 1
Average score
_____

POLICY AND POLITICAL INFLUENCES
1. Identifying relationships between influencing
   groups   5 4 3 2 1
2. Recognizing policy—informal and formal   5 4 3 2 1
3. Addressing ethical issues within the organization   5 4 3 2 1
Average score
_____

PUBLIC AND MEDIA RELATIONS
1. Understanding internal and external publics   5 4 3 2 1
2. Responding skillfully to media   5 4 3 2 1
3. Initiating positive publicity   5 4 3 2 1
4. Gathering public support   5 4 3 2 1
Average score
_____

Summation of Self-Assessment

Identify your five areas of strength (highest scores).

A.

B.

C.

D.

E.

Identify the five areas that you need to strengthen and list some strategies that might help you strengthen each area.

A.

Strategies to strengthen:

B.

Strategies to strengthen:

C.

Strategies to strengthen:

D.

Strategies to strengthen:

E.

Strategies to strengthen:

5

Learning From Pathfinders

Pretending that women and men are the same hurts women, because the ways they are treated are based on the norms for men. It also hurts men who, with good intentions, speak to women as they would to men, and are nonplussed when their words don't work as they expected, or even spark resentment and anger.

Tannen, 1990, p. 16

The outstanding women leaders interviewed for this book do not comfortably fit standard models of leaders often found in the literature. Many of them moved into high levels of administration much sooner than the accepted norm for women, a trend reported by Picker in 1980. These outstanding women share some similar traits yet are individually and wonderfully unique. Each has had many obstacles to overcome in finding her path to a top leadership position; each has been successful, however, in many different settings. Consistent with the research of Catherine Woo (1985), these women reveal an emotional toughness not commonly associated with women in the workplace. In addition, their motives for seeking positions of greater authority do not involve the search for power, per se, but rather, motivation stems from a need to have a positive impact on the lives of students and teachers.

This chapter focuses on disseminating responses from successful women administrators to the question, "What is your gut-level advice to women who wish to be educational leaders?" Their responses fall into four general categories: (a) education, (b) rewards, (c) "stick-to-itivity," and (d) support systems.

Education

The women made poignant comments about both formal and informal education. Much of the advice is what one would expect to hear about degrees and training; other advice is surprising and, occasionally, humorous.

The importance of a solid educational base cannot be emphasized enough. Almost universally, advice about formal education centered on pursuing doctorates and more. One superintendent's advice was, "Overcredentialize yourself" (compared to men and other women in the school, the district, the region, the state). Another said, "You've got to be good," and "You have to have some special talent." Special talent is interpreted as unique characteristics that serve the organization better than anyone else can demonstrate in similar settings. Developing special talent and being good, however, involve more than possessing innate talent. Modest talents and skills can be improved extensively through course work, teleconference attendance, conference presentations, and/or networking at local, state, national, and international levels. More specifically, course work and conferences at prestigious institutions have more clout than course work at a local college, unless a big name is the course professor or conference presenter. This is not to disparage local colleges but simply to identify the professional and personal growth and networking afforded by time and study in diverse locales.

An elementary school principal advises taking all possible course work regarding business and finance taught in business and education departments. This principal also advises extensive involvement in community activities. She serves on several large city and community boards and learns about financial matters from powerful business leaders who also sit on those boards. She gains insights into fund-raising and creative financing, useful strategies for her elementary school management.

Attending a variety of workshops and **reading constantly** in broad categories were strong themes in response to this request for gut-level advice. This area was reinforced by a superintendent: "Pay attention to issues and concerns and don't get hung up on gender. . . . Know laws, finances." Another superintendent stated ardently, "Know budget *and not just* curriculum." Yet another said straightforwardly, "Overcome budget phobia."

On a different level, some of the most visceral words of advice fall into what we have deemed the **informal education** category. Informal education, as here used, means operational strategies and attitudes. Here are some examples of advice for informal education:

If you are going to talk the talk, know the walk.

Women students need to be less subservient.

Don't speak out of both sides of the mouth.

Have an open mind and be flexible. Move away from, "Its always been done this way."

Don't separate yourself from male peers, colleagues, supraordinates, or subordinates; women need to become a part of, not separate from, the system.

Similar advice comes from another leader:

Press the flesh. By that I mean to become engaged in the dailiness of your craft. Pay attention to detail. Listen. Communicate.

Another woman said,

Get experiences with many people, add variety. See many roads; recognize your own gifts and talents and how they lead to a variety of choices.

And one strong piece of advice that supports what other women administrators have said is,

Think ahead. Be serious about thinking.

A different form of informal education involves modeling leadership with one's family. As succinctly put by one, "Tell your kids, 'I have to complete these tasks.' " The example of work ethic, determination, and conscientiousness establishes a firsthand example for the next generation.

In a similar mode, another administrator said, "Men must be trained to help solve the problem [the reluctance of some to accept women leaders]; society isn't ready for us through the front door."

Rewards:
Intrinsic and Extrinsic

Perhaps the quote that best summarizes the benefits of striving for and achieving high goals came with the affirmation that "being superintendent is the greatest job in the world; I wouldn't trade it for anything." Another administrator said simply, "There's a pot of gold at the end of the rainbow" (she was not necessarily referring to money). One woman said, "It is rewarding and motivating, helping people." Most superintendents interviewed indicated similar degrees of satisfaction.

When the demands of wife and mother are added, cautions are noted. Those cautions are similarly found in business literature chronicling the experiences of older women in schools who have tended to put off aspirations toward the CEO position until their children were grown or at least in secondary schools. Here's a sampling of quotations:

If you have a family, wait until the kids are grown.

When you move a lot and don't have a spouse, it gets lonely.

> Always think of family and self in terms of time factors. . . .
> You can really get bogged down in school work. Keep a per-
> spective on what's important.

In a more balanced perspective, perhaps, and toward a larger picture, a middle school principal said, "Be aware. Have both eyes open. Know yourself."

More than one superintendent expressed frustration about women who limit their horizons educationally and stop their career path at the level of principal or director. Perhaps the frustration is that more women do not understand that they can have a stronger influence on students' lives in other educational positions. These administrators seem to feel that the superintendency is not that much more difficult a position than being a principal but is much more rewarding. The superintendent receives the greatest monetary rewards in the school district but *primarily* is rewarded because, as the chief decision maker, she affects students' lives. The fallacious logic by some seems to be that many women will take positions of great responsibility in community service organizations (in fund-raising, complex budgeting, handling numerous organizational-logistical tasks, motivating other people to assist with various duties to get the job done) yet are reluctant to pursue top school executive positions requiring similar skills.

An elementary school principal in a large urban district referred to her role as principal as "like having a great big toy." In her elaboration, she was clearly interested in children having enjoyable and rigorous learning experiences, and she meant nothing frivolous or superficial by her analogy. She is recognized in her district as a very effective leader, quite unique and creative in her management of the schools to which she has been assigned. She has a great deal of autonomy in running her school, a trust that she has earned through her extensive efforts at making schools safe and enjoyable places of learning.

One woman administrator, in analyzing rewards in a holistic sense said, to those contemplating a move into administration, "Ask yourself, 'What is the cost?' and 'How can this change my family's life?' " She added that, in her experience, "Women consider these questions but men don't." Another administrator, in a holistic sense cryptically said, "Be willing to pay the price."

In terms of financial and emotional situations, one woman cautioned, "Men are rewarded on a different scale." She stated this as a fact of life for now, so to speak, but she hopes this is a temporary situation. She charges university faculty members, in particular, to be active in "impacting change." In some areas, data reflect changing policies toward pay for men and women in similar positions in different districts. In the state of Missouri, for example, women assistant superintendents are paid, on the average, $2,800 more per year than male assistant superintendents (Missouri Department of Elementary and Secondary Education, 1994). More dramatically, women at the level of director of secondary education receive, on the average, $7,000 more than males in similar positions. In fact, of the 25 categories of administrators in the Missouri report, mean salaries are higher for women in 11 positions, nearly half the total. It is noteworthy, however, that these 25 administrative categories represent a total of 2,666 males and 1,395 females. As is true in other settings and states, there are more females in higher paying suburban and urban districts than in smaller rural districts.

Stick-to-itivity

Stick-to-itivity is defined here as being creatively stubborn. It is informal—you can't really teach these things in a formal classroom setting. However, you can develop your own strategies and techniques by watching, analyzing situations, reflecting, and, most important, trying something different when the first attempt doesn't work.

Advice falling into this category reflects the most cryptic of responses:

Do it, but be aware. Have both eyes open.

If that is your goal, do it!

Don't give up when you don't get the jobs, keep trying.

Pursue whatever you want. Stay organized. Don't give up.

You have to prove yourself a little more. Things are going to continue to change.

"Work hard. Fight hard." In clarifying these remarks, it is clear that the words are meant to encourage. The theme seems to be a challenge to work toward difficult but rewarding goals, to persevere in situations that require thinkers. A secondary principal said, "We need risk takers, people willing to stand up and be counted. Education needs courageous women—and men." Several said that they know many women who would make excellent administrators, but the women don't seem to have confidence in themselves as being capable leaders.

In elaborating on her advice to not give up, one superintendent explained that she had been very successful in getting jobs *until* she first applied for a superintendency. She had several interviews and was a finalist several times before getting her first job as a superintendent. She said that the first rejection was a real blow because she had not previously experienced failure to any degree. But she wouldn't let herself get discouraged and accepted the situation as a new and more difficult challenge than she had ever experienced—a challenge that she could manage. She is now in her third superintendency, each move a better position. One woman, advising women how to meet challenges to leadership positions, said, "Don't blame others or attitudes; be honest, set goals, and be prepared." Another woman said, "Be sure you are willing to do what it takes to be where you want to be, . . . then consciously make the decision [to obtain your goal]." Still another said, "If you are questioning your ability, stop. Desire propels *if* the desire is there."

This may be a particular problem in certain Canadian provinces. In Manitoba, for example, one study revealed that women did not apply for principalships even when they were as well qualified as male applicants (Porat, 1985). In addition, according to an Alberta report, Porat continues, when women make it to the final list of candidates, they often do not present themselves as effectively as males in interviewing skills. One Alberta woman administrator in the study, however, reflects a difference from the norm. She was told from childhood on that she could do anything she wanted to do. She attributes her success as an educational leader to this nontraditional attitude.

One U.S. superintendent interviewee related a story exemplifying a tough situation that "any woman seeking a top administrative position must be able to handle." In a board meeting, she "stood up to a good ol' boy board member who shouts, harasses, intimidates, and once threw a pencil."

In summary, a final bit of advice from one interviewee, "You'll be great! Go for it!"

Support Systems

Women administrators consistently recommended that every aspiring female administrator should have personal as well as professional support systems. Most rely on family for personal support and colleagues (other, selected administrators) for professional support. One said simply, "Be solid in your personal life." Another said, "Always seek a balance of personal and professional life in order to stay nurtured as a human being." Yet another said, "Nobody is going to do it for you; you have to be your own support." In a specific scenario, one superintendent cautioned, "Don't go into a small male-dominated community and try to be the leader right away. Wait and let your strengths be known. Be grateful but don't lick boots." An elementary school principal was encouraging about the support received for her leadership efforts from her community in a very large city. She stated, "I've seen more gender bias on community boards than I have in education."

The women participating in our interviews all spoke of informal support systems, in addition to formal ones. That is, they talked more of colleagues whom they regularly telephone or meet for lunch, dinner, coffee, or drinks. Some said they deliberately avoid women's networks, finding those gatherings generally lacking in the support they need. Time is precious, and they use it well by developing their own support systems, if and when formal systems don't work for them. One top-level state administrator said that her experiences in women's networks in three states led her to avoid "bitch sessions" if at all possible. She will attend long enough to deliver an address, if asked, but finds commitments elsewhere to avoid the gripe sessions that always occur. One top-level administrator, in simple terms that speak volumes said, "Network nationwide. Attend seminars, workshops and conferences, seeking top administrators who are quality in attitude [for support]." Another said, "Speak with a united voice with other *good* women leaders." (Specific strategies for developing networks can be found in Chapter 7.)

Varia

Advice from one woman administrator does not fit exactly into any of the above categories but complements each: "Be enjoyable to be around and don't take yourself too seriously; laugh at yourself some." In addition, "Develop tough skin for hard decisions you must make."

One final bit of advice is certainly all-encompassing with wide translation, "Stay healthy."

6

Recognizing Mentoring Reciprocals

After interviewing exemplary women leaders in a wide range of states and provinces, recurring areas of expertise became apparent. Mentoring and networking are two essential practices that every participant developed to lesser and greater degrees. Like any effective skill, mentoring and networking require a concerted effort to perfect. Dimensions of each area and strategies to develop and refine these areas follow in this and the next chapter.

Mentoring

Simply stated, mentors guide, train, and support a less skilled or experienced person called a *novice, mentee,* or *protégé.* Recognition of the importance of mentoring for the development of individuals dates back to *The Odyssey,* with Mentor being the name of Homer's character who counseled and guided. The metaphorical odyssey continues in Daloz's (1983) article characterizing the three main functions of mentoring as (a) pointing the way, (b) providing support, and (c) challenging the mentee.

Mentoring has existed throughout history. Master instructing apprentice, Socrates guiding Plato, experienced teachers modeling for student teachers, doctors supervising interns, as well as myriad other relationships, exemplify the mentor/protégé relationship.

Hard and fast rules cannot govern any human interaction, including mentoring relationships. Age may have once been a standard factor, with the mentor being nearly a generation older. In new organizational structures and with varieties of emerging skills, such as in technology, it is not unusual to find a mentor younger than the protégé. Because women often enter administrative positions after raising children, their mentors may be supervisors or university faculty members who are younger than they.

Much of the literature reports that mentors and protégés are usually not related. Our interviews with exemplary women leaders, however, identified a great responsibility felt by these women to mentor their children. One participant stated that she even mentored her husband. Furthermore, when asked about who had mentored them, many women mentioned family members, including parents, husbands, and grandmothers.

The gender of the mentor or protégé of successful women administrators has also become a factor without any standard patterns found in the literature to date. Our interview findings support this trend. Women mentor and are mentored by both genders.

Learning Organizational Nuances

According to Kram (1983), mentorships enrich mentees by providing insights in two directions: (a) career dimensions and (b) psychosocial functions. Career benefits of mentoring are easily tabulated. From the mentor in one's work setting, the novice learns political realities, secrets of moving a project through the chain of command, techniques for dealing with the bureaucracy, ways to creatively budget, contacts throughout the narrow and broader community, and other survival techniques not written in any employee handbook.

For more experienced professionals, mentors can give career guidance for better moves to facilitate acquiring a goal within the organization or strategies for positioning oneself for long-term career objectives. For instance, full professors give assistant professors advice about writing and research agendas, important committee memberships, and other "hoops" necessary to gain tenure. Similarly, a superintendent can create situations for a principal with superintendency aspirations to attend the right meetings and conferences, pick the correct issues to champion, develop relationships with influential community members, and, in general, form an effective public relations campaign designed for positive and maximum visibility. Mentorships have the capacity to provide critical information that has been especially scarce in the orientation of women breaking ground in a new area or along a new path in a leadership role.

Psychosocial functions are often less distinct and probably not as overtly outlined by the mentor or the mentee. When the mentor supports, validates, and reassures, the mentee's self-confidence is enhanced and her or his outlook is improved. Psychosocial functions may be less definitive, but they are certainly as powerful as career guidance mentoring in affecting the novice's future.

Reciprocal Benefits

In the field of educational leadership, a telephone inquiry from a new principal about how a veteran principal managed to develop a business partnership in the community may lead to a mentoring relationship. Simultaneously, the new principal may be mentoring teachers with administrative aspirations. The veteran principal may have a mentor who is supporting his or her expertise in strategic planning. People are often concurrently mentors and mentees in very convoluted patterns.

Many benefits of mentoring relationships support mutual growth by both partners. Table 6.1 includes some commonly identified mutual benefits.

TABLE 6.1 Mutual Benefits of a Mentoring Relationship

Benefits for the Mentor	*Benefits for the Mentee*
Refining thinking	Safe sounding board
Rethinking	Establishing connections
Feeling good about supporting someone's growth	Insights into the history of the organization
Rejuvenation	Broader views
Reconnection	Balance and feedback
Feeling of worth	Safety net
Chance to pass the torch	Increased self-confidence

An additional advantage to the mentee was identified in a study by Fagenson (1988). Because mentees are somewhat protected and guided, they and other people in the organization perceive that the mentee has extended influence and power.

Employees, by being identified as mentors, feel greater job satisfaction and confidence in their roles in the organization because of the recognition. They also gather some of the energy and enthusiasm from their protégé who is just entering the profession. Daresh and Playko (1990b) describe the excitement that administrative mentors experience at being a teacher again.

Mentoring: An Essential for Women's Professional Development

Common sense conveys advantages of mentoring relationships for the development of both the mentor and protégé, and this has been borne out in a wealth of research. Hersi (1993), Turner and Thompson (1993), Astin and Leland (1991), and Hennig and Jardim (1978), as well as other researchers and writers, have established that mentoring is critical to female leadership development as well as to the probability of employment promotions. Mentoring enhances leadership development for both genders, but it is especially important for women because this has not been a long-standing part of career development for women.

Because, historically, women often exercised little control over their career paths, they did little planning and goal setting. Pregnancy or a spouse's job transfer could eliminate any career path, so it became less painful to not plan. Commonly, women relate stories about being in the middle of a graduate program and then they *"had to move."* Many women in their 50s and 60s still voice regret that they never finished various graduate degrees. Similarly, many women's stories recount being in position for promotion and moving from the area. Female internal locus of control is a new concept.

Because of pregnancy, growing children, or a partner's career, women have postponed planning and goal setting for a number of years. Hennig and Jardim (1978) noted that women make few career decisions and plan very little about their careers until later in their lives. Because women's careers are interrupted, secondly important, and/or started later in life, women lack a sense of how people receive advancements in their organizations. They are conditioned to think that hard work, good performance, and adding to their competence will necessarily allow them to advance.

Mentors become invaluable in explaining other essentials to advancement, such as how to increase one's visibility within the work setting. In school settings, women have gravitated to curricular and supervisory roles with low visibility and little opportunity to work with the power players in their system. Mentors can explain power structures and the carefully hidden movers and shakers.

With encouragement to develop career plans and professional goals, women need guidance to learn to discuss with, and garner support from their bosses for, their plans for advancement. Planning, positioning, and visibility have become critical skills for assisting employee promotion.

In our interviews of exemplary professional leaders, the women most often identified university faculty members as mentors. This is especially vital for career advancement when paired with findings by Mertz and McNeely (1990) that of the more than 100 women in their study of female educational administration faculty members, 62% were assisted in finding jobs by their major adviser.

Within our study, other groups were also identified as mentors. Next to university faculty members as the most commonly selected group, superintendents, followed by principals and district office administrators, were viewed as mentors.

A few interviewees responded that relatives, from parents to grandparents, had served as mentors. A grandmother-in-law was even mentioned. Spouses were cited as mentors by two interviewees.

When asked about who *they* mentored, participants identified people whom they supervised in some way, such as teachers, graduate students, student teachers, administrative interns, and principals. About one fourth of the interviewees reported mentoring young people: students in their schools, nieces and nephews, the children of friends, and their own children. Only one person felt that she mentored no one. The enriching nature of mentoring others was an often repeated sentiment. These leaders also recognized that occasionally they were unconsciously mentoring others by their example and random exchange.

Challenges With Gender Dimensions

Ideally, veterans seek out new employees to assist in a smoother beginning and orientation. First or "only" women in a setting experience isolation with no offers of mentoring or difficulty in approaching a mentor. Gender differences can make mentoring relationships awkward or so unique to the organizational culture that no experienced man is willing to risk making the first move. The relationship can be misconstrued as sexual (Bolton, 1980) or threatening to men who fear future losses of promotions to new organizational initiatives promoting women. To overcome any difficulties, cross-gender mentoring requires open communication about any gender discomfort.

Females mentoring males is important for all of the reciprocal benefits previously outlined. In addition, it is important to increase male understandings about women in professional roles as competent leaders.

With all of the benefits of other mentorships, females mentoring other females often establishes opportunities for pathfinders to pass along the heritage of their struggle gained along the way. Passing the heritage is soothing for both generations. Sagaria (1988) refers to the responsibility of women to cultivate leadership in other women as "generative leadership." Mentoring is a natural vehicle for generative leadership, and it facilitates learned pride in being a women. Nannerl Keohane (1991), President of Wellesley College calls this "a sense of connectedness with other women" (p. 607).

A negative "queen bee" syndrome identified by Bolton (1980) exists in some settings when the lone female resents and is threatened by other women moving through leadership ranks. Some of the interviewees reported learning to work with this phenomena. Most success was found when they assumed their leadership roles quietly and immediately solicited the advice and counsel of the queen bee. Recently, this roadblock has faded for two reasons: Professionals have a greater recognition of the reciprocal benefits of mentorships, and larger numbers of women in leadership positions have diluted most effects of the queen bee syndrome. Having more women in administrative ranks simply means there are now more people with an opportunity to mentor.

In our interviews of exemplary women leaders, we commonly found women principals mentoring women teachers. Interviewees often reported that they felt responsible to mentor other women *because there had been no one there for them.*

Mentoring as
Part of the Organizational Culture

Organizations variously embrace the concept of mentoring. Each organizational setting receives value from mentorships within the organization when skill levels are expanded, morale is increased, turnover is reduced, continuity is promoted, and professional development is achieved at minimal cost.

Mentoring relationships can be formally structured or serendipitous. Although support for a formal program is obvious through committed time and funding, organizational contexts also affect the growth of mentorships at the informal level.

Sometimes a small assistance with a minor project becomes a commitment on the part of a person with a skill to continue sharing with a novice. In fact, Luten (1991) found informal mentorships more effective than formal programs. The informal protégés identified greater career support, greater organizational socialization, and intrinsic job satisfaction.

A continuum from one extreme to another, with myriad approaches in between, represents organizational variation in support *or lack of it* for mentorships as an essential part of the organizational culture.

Cultures of Isolationism. In these systems, old traditions of isolated professionals still exist. Teachers, principals, and other educators are fully expected to do their jobs, follow policy, and keep quiet about problems as well as accomplishments. Collaboration is seen as a threat to the power structure. Competition is encouraged and even cutthroat among fellow employees.

Varieties Along the Continuum. Informal mentoring takes place in most systems. The climate in many schools and districts is naturally collaborative. Activities exist that stimulate interaction between professionals. Retreats, professional activities, team meetings, and similar events are planned not only to disseminate information but also to stimulate supportive behaviors. Some school systems have developed formal systems for beginning teachers and principals involving small support teams. Such a safety net often evolves into a long-term mentoring affiliation.

Cultures With Mentoring Interwoven Into the Fabric. Model programs have formal structures fostering mentoring relationships. For instance, mentoring is part of overall policy initiatives evident in Canadian efforts to increase the number of women in administrative positions. Young (1990) reports that in addition to affirmative action programs and special assignments, rewards for men and women who serve as mentors are included in this program throughout

Canada. School districts that make mentoring a priority conduct ongoing training so that individuals with already evident, identified, and screened collegial interpersonal skills can refine their mentoring skills. Release time is provided to support the mentor-mentee germination and development. Retreat-type opportunities exist to formulate goals and develop time lines for the partnership.

School districts and corporations throughout the country have identified the benefits of fostering professional development through formal mentoring programs. Increasingly, state departments of education are requiring that first-year teachers and principals be matched with more experienced educators or even with a small committee, providing more possibilities for a mentorship. Models of formalized mentoring programs have been formulated for local needs but have developed elements easily transferable to other settings. Through a simple inquiry, programs are usually generous with sharing their findings and format.

The Female Educators' Mentorship Project (Lynch, 1993) in Amarillo, Texas, formed because school administrators in the region did not represent the gender and cultural distribution of the district or the available pool of potential administrators. To support the development of underrepresented groups, a mentoring program was designed. Screening took place for selection of mentors and protégés into the yearlong program.

Activities began with a 2-day retreat outlining skills and responsibilities for each partner for the year. Other general and individual meetings as well as workshops followed. At the close of the formal project, a newsletter for linkage and informal assistance was put in place.

A variety of programs are needed for women aspiring to superintendency positions. Insights into this need were gained in a recent study of 24 women who had exited the superintendency (Tallerico, Burstyn, & Poole, 1993). The women surveyed identified that within-district mentoring programs become inappropriate and that opportunities in a wider region are needed. Women recognized that content and objectives needed to be more specific to the political, media-related, and broader demands of the superintendency. Although early-entry mentorships with exposure to general administrative skills are useful, superintendents require more esoteric help around political strategies, media approaches, coaching, broader funding dimensions, locating safety nets, and an opportunity to experience validation. The cliché "it's lonely at the top" is often true; thus additional supports are needed at levels comparable to business presidents.

Whether through formal or incidental means, organizations benefit by having mentoring partnerships as part of the system's culture. Cultures supporting mentoring promote communication, cohesiveness, continuity, understanding, and camaraderie, as well as improved employee motivation and satisfaction.

Stages of Mentorship Relationships

Mentorships, like other personal interactions, move through a variety of stages. Some works look at the progress as a three-stage interaction, but Matczynski and Comer (1991) consider five stages. Mentorships begin with careful selection and time for evaluating each other. Gehrke (1988) emphasizes that the selection must be one of mutual choice. This implies that many opportunities must be arranged for interchange before two people are comfortable and confident enough to become mentor and mentee. Mandated programs that, in effect, match pairs by drawing names from hats will have low rates of effective mentoring occurring.

The development of trust comes next. A clear understanding of each other is critical because of the nature of exchanges. For the mentee and mentor to be candid and honest with each other, trust must be implicit. Exchanges, advice, trying out ideas, and testing reflections require unhesitating trust.

By the third stage of the mentorship, the mentor is nurturing the growth of the mentee. The mentor makes suggestions for problem solving, strategies for visibility, and other positioning recommendations. The content exchanged goes beyond work advice and considers weightier issues. Gehrke (1988) deems such dialogue a "whole life vision" involving "helping the protégé to establish a view of how work fits into a whole life" (p. 45).

At the fourth level, mentors begin to intervene for mentees. They put their reputation on the line in backing the protégé for a significant task or committee assignment. The young bird, in effect, is trying her wings on her first short flight.

By the fifth level, the mentee begins disengaging and refocusing as an individual with the mentor close at hand as a safety net. As the protégé becomes more independent, both parties begin to feel some sense of loss as the relationship evolves to a supportive friendship role with less frequent encounters. At the final stage of the mentorship, the mentor actively sponsors and even campaigns for a promotion for the mentee.

A typical example of these stages can be seen by the evolution that occurs when experienced principals receive green assistant principals. Consider a district that in August had narrowed a field of over 200 applicants to 6 candidates as assistant principals. To determine which of the six schools would receive which candidate, the principals, as a group, spent 15 minutes talking with individual candidates and then convened a free-form question and answer period for all principals and candidates. A brief, informal reception followed. Afterward, each principal submitted his or her top choices to the superintendent for consideration.

One principal recalled making his selection on the basis of the person that he thought could move most quickly to help a severely overcrowded school. Without her even being aware of it, he immediately began to mentor the assistant. His first assignment was to have her ride each of the dozen bus routes that ran from migrant camps to trailer parks to country club communities. He had her monitor bus arrivals and departures as well as the lunchroom. Stacks of hundreds of free- and reduced-lunch forms were her responsibility to check and process. Because of these assignments, she quickly learned names and the diversity within a community new to her. By this point, she wanted to launch a project to bring the community into the school to support the reading program. He stood back and offered free reign.

Throughout the school year, she was temporarily taken to another school to assist another overcrowded situation. In so doing, she was balancing a variety of personal and professional decisions. The principal was accessible but never approached without invitation. When he conducted her formal evaluation near the end of the year, he joked that he hoped when she conducted his evaluation someday that she would be kind.

Within a week, she was transferred to become principal of a school embroiled in controversy. He continued to be available for advice when he was asked. Friendly calls were strategically placed when district report deadlines were approaching. They sometimes had lunch and conversed at administrative meetings and conferences. Their mentorship gradually evolved to a comfortable friendship. Without ever formally referring to the relationship as a mentorship, two educators grew.

If the principal had regarded the new assistant principal as a dumping ground for tasks he did not wish to handle, consider the difference in experience and growth. If he had embraced the "let them make it on their own" philosophy, neither the principal, assistant principal, nor the students would have benefited.

Strategies for Finding a Mentor

At some points in one's career, people need a mentor and do not wish to wait for serendipity to intervene in their career. In nonsupportive environments or a variety of other settings, women, new to administrative ranks or a specific position, often need to actively select and approach someone to mentor them. This is especially common when mentorships are not yet part of the organizational culture or when the woman is in the highest ranking position.

In seeking a mentor, one should begin with considering characteristics basic to anyone's being a good mentor. Common sense would dictate that a mentor should be someone with expertise and experience as an effective administrator in the setting or in a specific position. Mentors must be willing and positive about the benefits of supporting others. Furthermore, Daresh and Playko (1990a) point out that mentors must restrain themselves from telling how and, instead, ask the right questions. In their research, they found that mentors have to be open to other ways of approaching a problem or situation. Education is certainly an arena absent of one right way or one approach that will work in every situation. Finally, a mentor has to be sensitive to the emotional shifts endemic to school administration.

Because several factors deserve consideration in this important selection, careful analysis is warranted. The key people in each organization or in parallel positions in other districts or organizations should be considered. The following grid can assist decision making.

Possible Mentor Candidates

Place the names of possible candidates in the boxes across the top of Table 6.2 and rank each one according to the characteristics at the left. Rate them on a scale from 1 to 5, with 5 as ideal and 1 as unacceptable.

With the selection of the probable candidate, a simple direct request is appropriate. The mentee can outline what is hoped for in the mentorship. The discussion should leave comfortable openings for the selected person to bow out if she or he does not feel the time or situation is appropriate for assuming a mentoring relationship. If turned down, the mentee must realize that the decision is probably not a personal rejection. Time constraints are more than likely the issue.

Sometimes, an individual's reason for not accepting a mentoring role may not be one that he or she can discuss. For instance, there may be trouble in the school setting and the candidate's association might damage the mentee. Or the person may also have other career plans, and the timing is not ideal for beginning a mentoring relationship. In some situations, he or she may offer the name of another person who may be more suited to beginning a mentorship. Regardless, many people are very willing to work with novices in formal or informal mentorships.

Final Thoughts

The essential nature of mentoring is increasingly recognized. Initiatives to foster mentoring are being started by individuals and

TABLE 6.2 Candidates to Consider

NAMES									
Willing to help									
Time to help									
Wisdom about the setting									
Understands the power structure									
Is not threatened by me									
Respected by others									
Demonstrates mature thinking									

CHARACTERISTICS

small peer groups as well as by entire school districts. Interest and the need to know more is reflected in the fact that research is being conducted on every nuance of mentorships. Western Michigan University even sponsors the Mentoring Association, which publishes a newsletter entitled *The Mentoring Connection.* The National Association of Secondary School Principals and other professional associations offer training packages fostering mentoring as a basic administrative competency.

Through mentorships, "individuals are able to clarify their personal 'visions' of what educational leadership means, and also to develop a sense of commitment to a career in the field of administration" (Daresh & Playko, 1990b, p. 8). Mentorships allow both the mentor and mentee to gain a broader understanding of one's place in the profession as well as one's role within our culture.

7

![decorative bar]

Developing Networks

Networking is an inclusive concept covering a wide range of inter-actions among people. Melded into success-in-business pop culture, networking, regrettably, stressed who you knew as much as what was learned. The term *networking*, most recently mutated into the growing language of technology, emphasizes connections. Estab-lishing networks is an essential connection for anyone wanting to grow personally or professionally.

Johnson (1991) sees networking as a "tool for the construction of the future" (p. 5). Studies of women school board members iden-tified them as "part of a low-key, yet important and powerful, infor-mal network" (Marshall & Heller, 1983, p. 32). Greater awareness of the importance of networking and the effect of this tool has in-creased the probability that women will make the necessary effort to communicate with other professionals. Networking involves flex-ible structures of information sharing with a variety of people. Like friendships, networking requires commitment and organization.

Networking's Fit With Now

The popularity of networking has grown for several reasons. First, an information explosion has made it impossible for any individual to keep current on practically any single topic, much less on the universe of knowledge. Therefore, it becomes important to know who can help with answers or at least provide direction toward solutions.

Second, networking legitimizes social interaction with people. At the pace maintained by most working women, taking time to discuss ideas with others produces guilt. Social interaction is sacrificed as longer hours are logged at work. Demands of the professional and personal lives of women allow little unscheduled time. More than ever, a women's work is never done. Eating crackers at one's desk while shuffling papers and returning telephone calls easily replaces lunches that could be used for reenergizing with purposeful talk with others. Packed lives, therefore, make it necessary to schedule deliberate interactions. Networking helps bring some balance back to our lives.

Finally, networking mimics benefits created by mentoring while offering greater independence. In mentoring and networking, both givers and receivers prosper because of the relationship, information, and understandings generated. But in the larger circles created through networking, Swoboda and Millar (1986) conclude that networking is especially beneficial in helping women develop greater self-reliance and less dependency. Essential to passing along collective wisdom, the foundation developed through networking also supports increased confidence in one's leadership.

Overcoming the Historical Culture of Isolation

Since the era of the one-room school, teachers have been kept in relative isolation within their classrooms. Chances to talk with each other are rare and not encouraged in many school cultures. Teachers are expected to remain in their classrooms before and after school. In some districts, teachers are required to eat lunch isolated from colleagues. Space for common work and planning areas is not usually available. Such factors account for the findings by DeSanctis and Blumberg (1979) that the average duration of teachers' interactions with their colleagues is less than 2 minutes per day.

Recalling teachers' experiences during one's first year in the classroom, we find tales of trial and error, loneliness after most collegiate experiences, and little opportunity to dialogue with others for answers or feedback. Karge (1993), in examining correlations between school climate and beginning teachers' desire to remain in teaching, found that isolated environments are destructive. To retain enthusiastic, talented teachers, she concluded that it is crucial for beginning teachers to have a supporting network.

Until recently, models of how to plan together, share ideas, support each other, and strengthen teaching through professional collaboration were nonexistent. Rigidly constructed faculty meetings were stages for administrators to dominate time dispensing "administrivia." Real exchanges for problem solving were silenced. Seeking advice was a sign of weakness. Sharing ideas or success was viewed as showing off or not safe in immature school cultures characterized by hoarding and one-upmanship. Time to think about and to discuss one's teaching is often nonexistent.

Because the majority of educational administrators emerge from the teaching ranks, two changes must occur. New attitudes and skills must be developed to form networks and support systems within the work environments that they lead. Personally and professionally, it is also imperative to become part of a variety of networks.

Ways to Create Networks
in Schools and School Systems

Breaking schools' long-standing tradition of isolationism takes a vision of what is possible, fostered by the school principal and, ideally, district-level leadership. This changed notion is clearly summarized by Roland Barth (1990) in his phrase "schools as communities of learners" (p. 37).

Within Schools

Many practices in schools support collegiality. School administrators can ensure networking opportunities by being aware of some
basic practices. Some possibilities include the following:

- Schedule common lunch and planning times for groups of
  teachers.
- Examine the curriculum for places where collaborative team
  teaching could work with different numbers of students in
  meeting a variety of student needs.
- Develop, facilitate, and attend special interest groups on topics
  of concern to teachers and staff. When significant changes,
  such as integrating teaching blocks in a high school or creating a year-round calendar, are being planned, time will be
  needed for teachers to share concerns and knowledge.
- Promote study groups of teachers examining the latest professional literature and research.
- Develop problem-solving and sharing sessions.
- Provide for grade-level or departmental development and
  teaming as well as cross-grade and departmental interaction.
- Seize any opportunity for a celebration.
- Establish positive traditions.
- Find ways for socialization among the members of faculty
  and staff to occur.
- Encourage action research and establish time for activities
  and results to be shared.
- Schedule daily activities that foster interaction, and locate be-
  ginning teachers' classrooms so that they are not isolated from
  others.

Small efforts can result in large opportunities for networking. On
Wednesday afternoons at McCoy Elementary School, for example,
many extra cars and district work vans could be found. At student
dismissal time, the teachers' workroom became crowded with people
surrounding tables with large ditto paper boxes full of popcorn.
Teachers and staff started the tradition. Soon district supervisors and
work crews who found themselves on the southeast corner of town

on Wednesday dropped in. Great conversation and lots of humor surrounded the boxes of popcorn. If a professional development activity was scheduled, the boxes would arrive in the meeting area with a special smaller box for the facilitator.

McCoy Elementary School also had faculty and staff members who formed singing and dance groups for any occasion. The special surprise act at the end of the student talent show would always be the teachers performing. The celebration of the 25th anniversary of the school typified the camaraderie of the staff, with songs and dances interspersed with history lessons from the past 25 years.

Traditions and celebrations can be found in any school. They must be supported and fostered to convey the message that free exchange among members of the staff and faculty is important for them and, ultimately, important for establishing the type of school culture that produces the best possible learning for students.

Within School Districts

Networking opportunities for administrators must also be established and supported by school districts. The U.S. Department of Education (1992) in their resource manual, *Strengthening Support and Recruitment of Women and Minorities to Positions in Education Administration,* emphasizes the responsibilities of districts and other agencies to provide time and support for professional networks. They outline the need to establish networking meetings or opportunities to network within the context of other events.

In Arizona, a program was begun to specifically prepare women to assume principalships (Metzger, 1985). The Castle Hot Springs Program recruited women with principalship aspirations and potential nominations from superintendents and other administrators. As well as emphasizing basics such as interview skills, the program provided time for goal setting, stress management, and networking. Networking throughout and beyond the program strengthened the breadth of competencies that each participant held.

Each district can provide networking opportunities for administrators through professional development activities as well as other initiatives. With minimal expense, informal programs can be made available to encourage educators with promotion aspirations to set goals, visit or work in a variety of schools, and develop networks. A more organized approach to accomplish this task is often referred to as "teachers as leaders."

The teachers as leaders concept has become a growing movement sponsored by leading school districts and colleges of education. Groups of teachers are brought together on some type of regular basis to expand their skills and leadership experience. It is an excellent district effort to support networks and the professional growth of teachers.

The actual structure of teachers as leaders programs takes on a variety of approaches. Some districts sponsor summer institutes or conduct seminars in conjunction with professional development efforts throughout the school year. One program in Johnson City, Tennessee, grew from a collaboration with East Tennessee State University in forming a yearlong program of joint activities divided into three cycles (Hill & Simmons, 1993).

Within Cycle A, teachers worked through simulations and other activities to assess their leadership skills. They formed an individual educational plan around the assessment results. In small groups, they examined case studies and formed action plans for solutions. They simulated conflict situations to strengthen their verbal and nonverbal communication skills. They shadowed administrators and wrote about and shared their reactions. After collecting data from time studies on principals, they analyzed the information and compared it to classical and contemporary research findings. Visiting educational authorities who stimulate thinking and discussion were invited to meet or have lunch with the group. Some participants began exploring possibilities of networking with each other and university resources through E-mail. Throughout each cycle, participants developed a log of reflections and assembled a portfolio of readings and assessment information. Cycle B involved internships during the summer with monthly gatherings for reflecting and sharing experiences. Cycle C expanded the horizons of participants by determining how to study power structures within organizations. Small groups then conducted studies. Community and county influentials were interviewed and shadowed and, when possible, met with the group. After a session concerning proactive leadership to foster safe schools, teams of participants examined their school settings and generated recommendations. Cycle C also emphasized regional cultural activities and cultural diversity experiences. Feedback from teachers following the program included the following comments:

> I enjoyed meeting and working with others across the system. I gained from their perspectives.

> I really believed our system acted in a very fragmented style. As I have studied new leadership philosophies, observed various leaders in action, and watched decisions being made, I realized that we were not as separated as I had felt. In fact, our system seems to be trying to follow new trends but maybe is struggling a bit in some areas. Educators need to ask more questions, take a few more risks, and try new ideas.

> I have gained a desire to move more quickly in the change process to meet the needs of our students.

> I have gained a little more insight into myself and into the things that I feel and believe. There are others that also feel and believe as I do.

Another structure for developing a program in teacher leadership is sponsored by the Massachusetts Academy for Teachers (Teitel & O'Connor, 1993). A 2-week summer session is held to develop action plans for participants to put in place during the year. The 125 teachers in the program continue to meet on Saturdays during the school year with a focus on teacher renewal and the expansion of skills in six leadership strands, including mentoring, technology, educational policy, curriculum development, teacher research, and initiating change.

A more expensive but rewarding technique involves actual release of teachers from their classrooms. Lieberman (1988) reviews a program in which the district makes a commitment to relieve a number of teachers of their teaching duties for 1 year to work with other teachers on professional growth.

Teachers as leaders programs can be structured in a variety of ways. Regardless of the structure, several benefits are common to any teachers as leaders program. Benefits for teachers include the following:

- Teachers receive a chance to expand their network of friends and professionals.
- Time is provided to discuss and reflect on one's practice.
- A broader view of education is gained by looking at district, state, and national educational issues.
- Excellence in teaching is revisited.
- Opportunities exist to clarify one's vision of teaching, of good schools, and good school cultures (Rogus, 1988).
- Power structures become clearer and approachable.
- Skill is gained in decision making, communication, inquiry, problem solving, and other leadership competencies.

Benefits for school districts include these three:

- The vision of the district is more broadly communicated.
- Future administrators can be identified.
- Teachers become empowered.

Within Graduate Programs

Just as in schools and school districts, educational leadership preparation programs should also recognize the importance of networking as a practice that enhances any professional. Many educational leadership preparation programs have restructured their approaches to foster more student collaboration, discourse, reflection, and connections. Courses especially for women educational leaders are being designed at many universities.

The Women's Institute, a weeklong course taught each summer at the University of South Carolina, is a fine example (Tonnsen, Pigford, Jenkins, & Turner, 1992). During the week of the program, activities flow from early each morning until late in the evening. Facilitators are very aware that intense time together fosters networking. To promote other interactions, time for conversation is created by social functions following guest speakers. Seminar sessions are also purposefully constructed to allow speakers and past attendees interaction with each summer's new participants.

Other changes are occurring. Visions of past graduate programs with passive students in separate seats within carefully arranged rows being lectured to are disappearing. Specifically, grouping of students into cohorts and expanded acknowledgment of the concomitant benefits of carefully sequenced field experiences are two practices supporting educators' networking.

Cohorts, in this sense, are groups of students who move through graduate programs together. They may take a large part or all of their course work together. Beyond the physical proximity exists a commitment from these graduate programs to actively develop the cohort into a collaborative team. The immediate program goal is that educational leaders learn to network with aspiring leaders during graduate school for support and greater academic strength. At a second level, the hope is that these relationships will continue beyond graduation. On a still broader level, if these educational leaders learn to network in the graduate setting with this group, they can transfer their experience to other educational settings.

The cohort experience benefits students in several ways. The support and motivation from fellow members was the strongest factor supporting cohort membership according to surveyed participants (Hill, 1992). For women, the cohort model fits their needs and preferences for affiliation during the learning process (Shrewsbury, 1987). Students feel that they have academic support to excel.

Barnett and Caffarella (1992) outlined networking as an instructional technique that should weave through the curriculum in the educational leadership graduate cohort model. They saw networking, along with reflective seminars, reflective journal writing, life mapping, and other techniques, as essential to addressing issues of diversity with adult learners. In other words, if gender, ethnicity, and social class are to be understood, these issues must be dealt with on many levels by people being trained as future educational leaders.

Field experiences, ideally, are integrated throughout any graduate program in educational leadership. Transition for moving from

PROFESSIONAL AND SELF-DEVELOPMENT

confidence and experience. Field experiences assist this process. Experiences begin with planned observations, time studies, shadow-
ing, interviewing, and other interactions scaffolding to the more
detailed and intricate internships (Hill, 1994b). Time to reflect and
analyze what is seen and what impressions are gathered is essential
to professional development. Graduate programs preparing leaders
for tomorrow's schools are experiencing rapid shifts. The nature of
many of the new practices and the wide changes in philosophy are
especially potent for female graduate students. As the image of the
professor shifts from all-knowing to facilitator, students are empowered. Students are becoming part of the decision-making process by
having choices in program content, class scheduling, course curriculum, and other long-standing, rigid pillars of "the ivory tower."

Consider the implications for women who, in the past, went to
graduate school and found the male dominant/female subservient
framework they had known in their homes as children and later in
society's expectations of them as married. After dealing with some
fear and discomfort over having options that were never there,
women in these programs are now encountering relative degrees of
exhilaration and freedom.

Within Professional Associations

Professional associations have long been an important part of
networking for educators. Many have histories of being closed so-
cieties for women, first in membership and for years later, in
leadership. Interestingly, those organizations are often the ones
presently struggling for membership. Several dynamic professional
associations have become aware that one of their major services is
serving as a catalyst for networking. For instance, annual conferences are a critical setting for participants to discuss issues and talk
with each other. Entire conferences with formats of being talked *to*
have largely ended. From local to state to national levels, these organizations can, and often do, provide settings for true discussions
of the essence of education.

Strategies for Personal Networking

For personal growth, renewal, and stimulation, it is important that we each participate in a variety of different networks (Duvall, 1980). Social, intellectual, and in-depth interactions with others should not be limited to work circles. These encounters are sometimes thought of as homes. Emotionally healthy people have several members of both their cognitive and emotive homes. We share thoughts and ideas with members of our cognitive homes and emotions and feelings with members of our emotive homes. Networking helps establish trusted members of these homes, giving us balance, perspective, insights, and awareness.

In a study of 75 female managers in business and education, Funk (1987) found that the greatest sacrifice managerial women make is giving up time with family, friends, and self. The pace of the lives of most professional women requires that networking be added to the schedule. Time for sustaining one's cognitive and emotive homes requires purposeful effort.

An example of one woman's network involved a briefly existing book review group jokingly called the Ladies Literary Guild, LLG for short. They met a few times on Saturdays over 5 or 6 months in 1981. The husband of one member, in his early 30s, died unexpectedly in an airplane accident. The group pulled together to provide the extended family often missing in the melting pot communities of the migrant middle-class common in Florida, California, and Texas.

At the time, everyone in the LLG was an elementary school teacher. Only a couple of members are still in Florida, and only a few still teach. Other members have since become editors at publishing companies, self-made computer entrepreneurs, and professors. Marriages have come and gone, with a renewed support group often rallying during divorces. Through the years, many of the LLG still make efforts to see each other and hold ad hoc reunions. Reflecting back recently, some members realized that one of the largest benefits of the group coincided with the timing of other life events to stimulate and increase consciousness and newly discovered pride about being women.

Regardless of the vehicle, networking is important for perspective and growth. The following list contains examples of strategies for networking that can be incorporated into anyone's crowded calendar:

- Schedule lunch one day a week for sharing ideas with someone.
- Plan a book review session one Thursday a month with a diverse group of women.
- Organize a biking, hiking, rafting, or canoeing outing one Sunday a month.
- Meet with key contacts at the same annual professional conference.
- Make a self-commitment to telephone at least two inspiring and insightful contacts a month.
- Use fax, Internet, Bitnet, or whatever electronic means to send a rotating newsletter to friends on general topics of news or on a specific growth area. As each person receives it, he or she adds a comment, item, or an entire outline and sends it back to the network.

New in Town Networking

In our mobile society, being new in town and knowing no one is not uncommon. Starting a new network usually begins with circles from one's work setting. Most educators are gregarious and quickly get to know other people in their work settings. Professional educational associations are another good place to begin. Locate the local chapter of Kappa Delta Pi or Phi Delta Kappa and attend their meetings. The American Association of University Women is another organization with objectives and activities that are comfortable and stimulating to new residents. Locating the next meeting time and place can be a good excuse to begin conversations with people who are part of other networks already functioning within the community.

For broader community views, service organizations are important ways to serve while gaining acquaintances in your network beyond people within your work setting. Service organizations such as Rotary, Kiwanis, Optimists, or Lions clubs now warmly welcome women in most chapters. Their community service goals are important and a fine place to spend some time.

Sports of many types provide the pivotal point for a variety of local organizations. Golf has lost its male dominance. Many courses gladly pair a single player with others for a round. Recreation clubs are another comfortable setting for meeting people.

Final Thoughts

The need to effectively network has spawned millions in sales for business cards, pocket address computers, simple to elaborate systems for filing business cards, and a vast array of other battery, solar, or manual ways to organize networks. Information highways, known variously as E-mail, Internet, Bitnet, and others, move networking into a new generation.

Networking can enhance one's knowledge base, extend social interactions, and provide support on achieving career goals. Funk's 1987 study of 75 female managers in business and education analyzed the sources of stress they found and the coping mechanisms that they used. Major sources of stress centered around lack of time and constant deadlines coupled with family responsibilities and traditional female roles. Solutions for these dilemmas involved learning to be team players through collaborating and cooperatively enjoying other female successes. Crucial to this growth is the development of support systems within and outside one's family.

Gail Stephens, Deputy Executive Director of the American Association of School Administrators, shared her insights on how to grow professionally. She advises women to network with other women, ask questions and seek advice, get the most and best training, become involved in professional meetings and associations, and not waste time trying to change a district that is blocking women from administrative promotion (Rist, 1991).

Women in administrative roles get labeled as extremely competent or incompetent. There is no middle ground. Surveys of female educational administrators in Oregon in 1980 (Erickson & Pitner, 1980) repeat advice heard from many corners. These administrators suggest that women must dialogue with male coworkers, make opportunities to speak, build a network of contact, find a mentor, and increase their visibility to achieve the success they are seeking.

8

![separator bar]

Exploring Paths

Are there common paths along which successful women educational leaders progress? Is there a formula for others to follow? What have women leaders learned from the paths they have taken? The 34 women interviewed in our study responded to queries attempting to determine answers to these questions.

Much can be found in the literature that summarizes career paths of men and women educators; none of the outstanding women leaders interviewed for this book, however, fit the mold as presented in the literature to date. For the purposes of this chapter, individual paths are discussed, rather than attempting to find a single, typical path representative of this group of outstanding women leaders. By detailing individual paths, it is hoped that readers will more readily identify with one or more examples, rather than feeling left out if their particular career paths to date are not on target with the "norm." In other words, there is now no norm in terms of job sequencing to reach top levels of school leadership, at least for the women leaders interviewed for this book.

Degree Paths of Interviewees

The range in ages for interviewees' receiving a bachelor's degree is 20 to 30 years, with a mean age of 22.31. The most frequent age is 21 (34%). The next closest age is 22 (31%). This is somewhat younger than the mean age for a combined sample of men and women administrators as found by Pavan and D'Angelo in 1990. In examining this data, it may be good news for some readers that neither early nor relatively late entry into teaching has much bearing on the chances for moving through the ranks to leadership positions.

These outstanding women leaders spent fewer years than the norm for other researchers in classroom teaching positions prior to obtaining their first administrative positions. For example, in 1990 Pavan and D'Angelo found that their group of male and female administrators spent on the average, 10 years as classroom teachers before obtaining their first administrative position. Others (Dopp & Sloan, 1986) have found that women usually spend 15 years in the classroom and men 5 years before moving into administration. However, the mean number of years teaching for the current group of interviewees is 8. The most *frequently occurring* number of years of classroom teaching for this group of women leaders is 5, followed by 3 years, then 2 years.

The range in ages reveals that some of the women chose to wait for applying for administrative positions until their children were in school; some even waited until their children were in college. Other women, however, chose to seek assistance with child care from family or professionals so that they could have more time to devote to their careers at a younger age.

The range in ages of interviewees at the first administrative position is 22 to 49 years. The most frequent age is 30, with a mean age of 33.6. Again, this is different from what some prior researchers have found. Pavan and D'Angelo (1990), for example, reported that, on the average, women in their study received their first administrative positions at a mean age of 36.0. Of the current women interviewees, 40% received their first administrative position at the age of 30 *or younger.* The wide range in ages (22-49) of the current interviewees reflects that, like the women in prior research studies, some chose to wait until their children were older before applying for the first administrative position. They all were successful in obtaining those positions, so it seems reasonable to assume that they could have moved through the ranks sooner, *if they had so chosen.*

Educational Paths of Interviewees

There is no discernible pattern of *undergraduate* majors in examining the career paths of these outstanding women leaders. Undergraduate degrees represent elementary education, home economics, special education, physical education, and virtually all of the liberal arts. The commonality is that all 34 began their educational careers as classroom teachers.

Master's degrees, however, fall primarily into the categories of administration, with some degrees in guidance and counseling and curriculum. A few of the interviewees have master's degrees in specialized areas of reading, special education, English, and speech communication, but again, there is no overwhelming representation of a particular discipline reflected in the master's degrees of interviewees. In addition, some interviewees hold specialist degrees in educational administration.

More commonalities emerge with the terminal degree. Doctorates are in educational administration and supervision, as would be expected, with some indicating near-equal course work in curriculum.

Early Work Experience

The only commonality of early work experience (prior to teaching) is a strong work ethic. Work experience reflects a wide variety of jobs. Only some of the jobs held prior to earning bachelor's degrees reflect work with children: tutoring; lifeguarding; and serving as camp counselor, playground supervisor, or swimming instructor. Other interesting jobs that do not, however, involve interactions with children include detasseling corn; modeling; dog sitting; working in furniture sales; and working as a nurse's aide, typist for an architect, mail carrier, "gofor" for a cannery, cocktail waitress, or farm worker (baled hay, milked cows, and skinned hogs).

Career Paths in Education

There is no typical career path—no sequence of positions that reflects a generalized pattern within this group of women leaders. Although all began their educational careers as classroom teachers, 5 then moved to school counselor positions, and 6 moved out of the classroom to teaching fellowship-type positions while pursuing graduate degrees as full-time students and university-level instructors. Three of the women moved into principalships for their second positions, but only 2 moved into assistant principal positions for their second job. Other second positions include reading specialist, resource teacher, director of a private school, a position in the state department of education, homemaker, gifted education teacher, deaf education teacher, community college instructor, and non-teaching (private business) work.

Thus, for this group of women leaders, pursuing graduate degrees was the single most common option after their experiences as classroom teachers. This is different from findings by Pavan and D'Angelo (1990), Dopp and Sloan (1986), and Shakeshaft (1989), indicating the secondary principalship as the most frequent position held prior to superintendencies.

The following is a sampling of career paths (after teaching) of the women interviewees who achieved positions as superintendents:

- Counselor-assistant principal-principal-superintendent
- Doctoral fellow-elementary principal-high school principal-superintendent

- Special education teacher-counselor-director of special education-superintendent
- Noneducation job-research associate/college instructor-assistant principal-director of curriculum-principal-assistant superintendent-superintendent

Would They Do It All Again?

In response to the question posed to all interviewees, "Would you take the same path again?" most interviewees answered in the affirmative, with a few qualifications. Many indicated that they would have liked to move "up the ladder" sooner, but they felt the climate for women administrators was not right. Some said they wished they had moved regionally sooner to accept promotions, and others said that, in retrospect, they would have gone for graduate degrees sooner. *Only one* replied "probably not." She is now thinking about retirement and has several moves within her career affecting vesting in retirement systems, although she has held several positions of great responsibility and does indicate a great deal of satisfaction in her professional accomplishments.

The job satisfaction and success expressed by this group of interviewees is consistent with the research of Dopp and Sloan (1986). The majority of women superintendents in their survey indicated that they learned in their first administrative positions "that they were stronger and more capable than they had imagined" (p. 123). Specifically, they referred to "interpersonal skills and competencies necessary for success" (p. 123) as school leaders. Of the superintendents in that study, 50% indicated that their gender did not hinder their career success, once they had been selected for the first administrative position. Furthermore, the majority of the administrators in that study believed that demonstrated competence was the major factor in reaching upper levels of administration. In addition to interpersonal skills, that group of superintendents stressed the importance of developing financial expertise. (Gaining financial expertise was a recommendation from the interviewees in partial response to the question about gut-level advice in Chapter 5.) The capabilities demonstrated through interpersonal and financial skills led to the statements of overall job satisfaction for both the current interviewees and those represented in the Dopp and Sloan study.

Mobility Issues

Although many of the interviewees felt they could have moved "up the ladder" sooner if they had moved geographically, not one of the interviewees negotiated a job for her spouse so that she could accept a better position in a different location. Furthermore, only one interviewee indicated that she and her husband rotate moves. In this regard, educators appear to be more conservative than women in business. A recent CNN report (*CNN Business News*, May 21, 1994), for example, indicated that more and more couples are now moving so that the wife can accept a job with more responsibility and pay, with husbands agreeing to search for positions in the new locale.

Dopp and Sloan (1986) discuss a report by the American Association of School Administrators about women in public school administration. Their conclusion is that lack of geographical mobility strongly affected the women in that research. However, personal factors such as marital status, number of children, and ages of children did not significantly affect the upward career mobility of women in administration. More and more possibilities appear available to women in school administration, particularly if given the opportunity to relocate.

Issues of Child Care

Shakeshaft, in 1989, pointed out that although men have often been freed from their military obligations to serve out their public school obligations, rarely have they been granted paternity leaves so that heir wives could serve out their public school obligations.

Those in the current group of women educational leaders do indicate *some* changes in spousal and school support for family obligations. A recent article supports this finding. The August 18, 1994, *The New York Times* feature article by Schwartz, "Daddy's Home," carries the lead, "More women are insisting on fatherly participation, and more men are accepting the role"[1] (p. 4). The article, based on Pepper Schwartz's (1994) book, *Peer Marriage: How Love Between Equals Really Works,* contains a series of recommendations about how couples can more equally balance home and child care responsibilities.

We predict that the trend in business for more males to become involved in child care will have a positive influence on the educational community in support of more balanced child care obligations. The Association of Teacher Educators (ATE) Committee on Gender Equity is only one example of many educational organizations that have strong commitments in supporting women as educational leaders. (Note: The ATE membership is composed of public school as well as university-level educators.)

Sacrifices

When asked, "What sacrifices have you made because of your path selection?" a variety of responses, some expected and some unexpected, were given. The most candid reply may best reflect the tenor of this category: "I learned you can't be a good teacher, [administrator], mother, and f—— in the same day. I've had less quantity but I hope more quality with my daughter; my husband took on a lot of parenting [which wasn't a problem]."

Some of the women expressed varying degrees of regret for lost family time, as well as lost time for self, particularly with hobbies. Many indicated that they spend 11 to 14 hours a day on the job and, often, longer on days with faculty meetings and/or PTA or school board meetings.

Gender Bias?

To explore perceptions of gender bias, all the interviewees were asked, "Have you ever been sexually harassed?" Only 7 replied "No." Three of the women replied, "No, not really," which seems to indicate a degree of harassment as interpreted by someone else, perhaps, but nothing that they feel was at a level to cause them a problem. Other replies were "What woman hasn't?" "Yes, that's a part of life; no big deal." "Nothing overt." "Of course." "Yes, but nothing [I] couldn't handle." "Sure." "Yes, by some standards, but I wasn't aware of it at the time." "Yes, before knowing what it was. Since then, [I] share a book on harassment with those who need it."

Sharing a book on harassment with those who need it may be the most positive proactive response of all. Responses such as "Not really," "Yes . . . no big deal," and "By some standards" may indicate a form of passive acceptance or denial of a very insidious phenomenon that many women leaders experience. These responses may indicate that administration preparation programs need to be much more assertive with both men and women students in educating about sexual harassment. Many men, unfortunately, still do not realize that their lifelong habits of calling all women in the workplace "Hon" or "Babe" is demeaning.

The research of the American Association of University Women (AAUW), the Sadkers (Sadker & Sadker, 1993) and others in this area is desperately needed. The AAUW (1991) report *How Schools Shortchange Girls*, for example, revealed that students in middle school and high school are very aware of gender bias:

> Students were asked, "Are there any policies, practices, including the behavior of teachers in classrooms, that have the effect of treating students differently based on their sex?" One hundred percent of the middle school and 82 percent of the high school students responding said "yes." (p. 82)

In their ensuing report, *Shortchanging Girls, Shortchanging America: A Call to Action*, the AAUW (1992) reports the founding of the Initiative for Educational Equity to focus efforts on America's national agenda with the goal of eliminating gender bias in education. The report describes a January 1991 meeting in which AAUW findings were presented to an Educational Equity Roundtable of educators, business people, public officials, and perhaps most important, the media. The result was "an overwhelming commitment by the leaders to address the needs of girls and young women . . . to combat gender bias . . . to seek solutions at the local, state, and national levels" (p. 5).

Leisure Activities

With these women indicating 12+ hour workdays, it was anticipated that few leisure activities would be identified, but they play as hard as they work. In response to the question, "What do you do for fun?" the answers were just as diverse as in other areas. Some typical responses included the following: "Go to movies, read, walk, swim." "Travel, run, be with people and laugh, walk." "Church." "Play tennis, attend plays and concerts." "Fish, swim, various [several] community groups." "Perform music, ride motorcycles." "Bicycle, garden, gourmet cooking, junk reading." "Golf, curling, needlework." "Relaxation techniques, walks on the beach." "Snorkeling, target shooting." "Dance by myself." "Listen to opera, collect art, participate in a think tank on current social issues." "Family time. Went paintballing recently."

In summary, whatever gives release from the stress of the job is relaxation, even if it involves intensive activity and lengthened days.

The Superwoman Syndrome?

After the women described incredibly complex work days and myriad leisure activities, the question posed was, "Are you a superwoman?" Not one of the interviewees replied with a straight "yes" without qualifiers. Most indicated that probably someone else would say so, and quite often, they added that they see that tendency as negative and are trying to lead more balanced lives these days. Some indicated that they are trying to be less of a superwoman by relying on a spouse who helps with household duties in addition to having a weekly or monthly cleaning lady. One candid reply reflects the sum of the other women's responses: "Hardly that, but I am independent, energetic, tough, sensitive, thoughtful, organized, vivacious, knowledgeable and get bored with dysfunctional power structures."

The average person on the street may view that response as coming from an obvious superwoman, but that's the point! These outstanding women leaders are not typical; they are special. They have been very diligent and driven, perhaps, to reach the goals they set. Being a woman in a leadership position, particularly the superintendency (the U.S. equivalent to director), is still not the norm in North America. However, for those willing and ready to set that position as a goal, it is achievable and very satisfying. (At this point, if you have not already done so, we recommend that you assess your own leadership competencies with the Chapter 4 guidelines.)

It is hoped that the career paths of this group of outstanding women leaders will encourage other women to seek administrative positions. Because there is no magic track to top positions, the time is right for women at any level of their educational careers to seek advancement. Several other researchers (Dopp & Sloan, 1986; Feistritzer, 1988) have found that superintendents and principals—women as well as men—have a high degree of job satisfaction. More women should be encouraged to pursue those positions.

Addendum:
Planned Affirmative Action

Individual initiative is well and good, and in some cases, enough. More support from leaders at local, state, and national levels would be even better. Women have proven their capabilities to be excellent educational leaders; however, tradition and bias still limit their efforts in many ways. If local school district boards of education, as part of their strategic long-term plans, develop and implement guidelines for increasing the number of women in administration, such efforts should only help women interested in leadership positions. Furthermore, because of the interaction of male and female teachers with administrators in decision making, usage of site-based management in public schools would be a more appropriate setting than the top-down administrative models still used in many schools. More interaction = more opportunity to observe women in action as leaders.

Often, it has been reported that when women receive letters of rejection for hiring for administrative positions, lack of experience is cited as the main reason they were not hired. However, many times, males with less or equal experience are hired to fill those roles. More monitoring of such activity by some sort of watchdog organization could help to keep school boards aware of such discriminatory practices. Hiring of women administrators seems to be the biggest incentive for other women in seeking administrative positions. The greater variety of strategies to employ in supporting women as leaders, the greater the opportunity for reaching more qualified women leaders.

Susan Scollay (1994) encourages school boards to be proactive: Require that all district reports include gender as a variable of analysis, learn the specifics about state and federal laws regarding gender discrimination, and exert strong leadership in developing a team approach with other school administrators and school board members. In so doing, according to Scollay, "You can help ensure for your daughters, nieces, and granddaughters a more equitable education than your sisters, aunts, and mothers received" (p. 48).

Conclusion

The 35 women educational leaders interviewed reveal that although obstacles exist, it is possible for women to move into administrative positions at varying ages and with varying degrees of experience and expertise. We encourage other women to also seek those positions.

Note

1. Copyright © 1994 by The New York Times Company. Reprinted by permission.

References

Aburdene, P., & Naisbitt, J. (1992). *Megatrends for women.* New York: Villard.

American Association of University Women. (1991). *How schools shortchange girls.* Washington, DC: Author.

American Association of University Women. (1992). *Shortchanging girls, shortchanging America: A call to action.* Washington, DC: Author.

American Association of University Women. (1993). *Hostile hallways: The AAUW survey on sexual harassment in America's schools.* Washington, DC: Author.

Andrews, R. L., & Basom, M. R. (1990). Instructional leadership: Are women principals better? *Principal, 70*(2), 38-40.

Astin, H. S., & Leland, C. (1991). *Women of influence, women of vision.* San Francisco: Jossey-Bass.

Auel, J. M. (1980). *The clan of the cave bear.* New York: Crown.

Barnett, B. G., & Caffarella, R. S. (1992, October). *The use of cohorts: A powerful way for addressing issues of diversity in preparation programs.* Paper presented at the annual meeting of the University Council for Educational Administration, Minneapolis, MN.

113

Barth, R. (1990). *Improving schools from within*. San Francisco: Jossey-Bass.

Bill would require release of athletic expenses. (1994, August). *Higher Education and National Affairs*, p. 2.

Bolton, E. B. (1980). A conceptual analysis of the mentor relationship in the career development of women. *Adult Education, 30*(4), 195-207.

Brathwaite, F. (1986). *The challenge for female educational leaders: An examination of the problem and proposed solutions through educational and social change strategies*. Synthesis paper for doctor of philosophy, Walden University, Minneapolis, MN.

Business News. (1994, May 21). Atlanta: CNN.

Crosby, F. J. (1991). *Juggling: The unexpected advantages of balancing career and home for women and their families*. New York: Free Press.

Daloz, L. (1983). Mentors: Teachers who make a difference. *Change, 15*(6), 24-27.

Daresh, J. C., & Playko, M. A. (1990a, September). Mentor programs: Focus on the beginning principal. *NASSP Bulletin*, pp. 73-77.

Daresh, J. C., & Playko, M. A. (1990b, April). *Preservice administrative mentoring: Reflections of the mentors*. Paper presented at the annual meeting of the American Educational Research Association, Boston.

Database. (1994, July 11). *U.S. News and World Report*, p. 12.

DePree, M. (1992). *Leadership jazz*. New York: Doubleday.

DeSanctis, M., & Blumberg, A. (1979, April). *An exploratory study into the nature of teachers' interactions with other adults in the schools*. Paper presented at the annual meeting of the American Educational Research Association, San Francisco.

Dopp, B. K., & Sloan, C. A. (1986, November). Career development and succession of women to the superintendency. *Clearing House, 60*(3), 120-126.

Duvall, B. (1980, November). *Networking*. Paper presented at the annual meeting of the Speech Communication Association, New York.

Edson, S. K. (1987). Voices from the present: Tracking the female administrative aspirant. *Journal of Educational Equity and Leadership, 7*(4), 261-277.

Eisler, R. (1987). *The chalice and the blade: Our history, our future.* San Francisco: Harper & Row.

Erickson, K. A., & Pitner, N. J. (1980, December). The mentor concept is alive and well. *NASSP Bulletin*, pp. 8-13.

Fagenson, E. A. (1988). The power of a mentor: Proteges' and non-proteges' perceptions of their own power in organizations. *Groups and Organizational Studies, 13*(2), 182-194.

Feistritzer, C. E. (1988). *Profile of school administrations in the United States.* Washington, DC: Center for Educational Information.

Feuer, D. (1988, August). How women manage. *Training*, pp. 23-31.

Flax, E. (1992, May/June). A time to mourn. *Teacher Magazine*, pp. 18-19.

Funk, C. (1987, May). *Female managers in business and education: Sacrifices, stressors, and support systems.* Paper presented at the Annual Conference on Women and Work, Arlington, TX.

Gehrke, N. J. (1988). On preserving the essence of mentoring as one form of teacher leadership. *Journal of Teacher Education, 39*(1), 43-45.

Grogan, A. (1993). Making up for lost time. *Women's VU, 16*(4), 1-2.

Hagberg, J. (1984). *Real power: Stages of personal power in organizations.* San Francisco: Harper.

Hammond, L. A., & Fong, M. L. (1988, August). *Mediator of stress and role satisfaction in multiple role persons.* Paper presented at the annual meeting of the American Psychological Association, Atlanta, GA.

Hammons, J. O., & Keller, L. (1990). Competencies and personal characteristics of future community college presidents. *Community College Review, 18*(3), 34-41.

Hennig, M., & Jardim, A. (1978). *Managerial woman.* New York: Simon & Schuster.

Hersi, D. T. (1993). Factors contributing to job satisfaction for women in higher education administration. *CUPA Journal, 44*(2), 29-35.

Hill, M. S. (1992, November). *Graduate cohorts: Perceptions of benefits and catalysts to cohesiveness.* Paper presented at the annual meeting of the Southern Regional Council on Educational Administration, Atlanta, GA.

Hill, M. S. (1994a). Emerging paths: Expanding definitions of educational leadership. *Connections, 2*(3), 3-5.

Hill, M. S. (1994b). Transitional supports for the internship. *DESIGN for Leadership, 4*(3), 1-2, 6.

Hill, M. S., & Hill, F. W. (1994). *Creating safe schools.* Thousand Oaks, CA: Corwin.

Hill, M. S., & Simmons, M. (1993). Teachers as leaders: Fostering future decision makers. *DESIGN for Leadership, 3*(3), 2, 8.

Jarvis, B. A. (1992). *A study of the relationship between teacher hardiness and job satisfaction at selected elementary schools.* Unpublished dissertation, University of Central Florida, Orlando.

Johnson, J. R. (1991, April). *Networking: How to permeate the glass ceiling—Some highlights from recent studies of networking among women.* Paper presented at the annual meeting of the American Educational Research Association, Chicago.

Jones, E. H., & Montenegro, X. P. (1982). *Climbing the career ladder: A research study of women in school administration.* Arlington, VA: American Association of School Administrators.

Karge, B. D. (1993, April). *Beginning teachers: In danger of attrition.* Paper presented at the annual meeting of the American Educational Research Association, Atlanta, GA.

Kelly, R. M., & Guy, M. E. (1991). Public managers in the states: A comparison of career advancement by sex. *Public Administration Review, 51*(5), 402-412.

Keohane, N. L. (1991). Educating women for leadership. *Vital Speeches of the Day, 57*(19), 605-608.

Kobasa, S. C. (1979). Stressful life events, personality, and health: An inquiry into hardiness. *Journal of Personality and Social Psychology, 37*(1), 1-11.

Kobasa, S. C., Maddi, S., & Courington, S. (1981). Personality and constitution as mediators in the stress-illness relationship. *Journal of Health and Social Behavior, 22*(4), 368-378.

Kosnett, J. (1992, June). The slow (and steady) growth of women's businesses. *Kiplinger's Personal Finance Magazine,* p. 16.

Kram, K. E. (1983). Phases of the mentor relationship. *Academy of Management Journal, 26*(4), 608-625.

Lawton, M. (1994, March 9). Female seniors in 1992 more ambitious than in '72, study finds. *Education Week,* p. 7.

Lieberman, A. (Ed.). (1988). *Building a professional culture in schools.* New York: Teachers College Press.

Lunenburg, F. C., & Ornstein, A. C. (1991). *Educational administration.* Belmont, CA: Wadsworth.

Luten, T. D. (1991). *A comparison of informal mentoring relationships and formal mentorship programs.* East Lansing: Michigan State University Press.

Lynch, H. (1993, May). Learning from the field: Mentoring projects in field-based settings. *Women's Educational Equity Act Publishing Center Digest.* Newton, MA: Women's Educational Equity Act Publishing Center.

Marshall, C. (1985). From culturally defined to self-defined: Career stages of women administrators. *Journal of Educational Thought, 19*(2), 134-147.

Marshall, C., & Mitchell, B. A. (1989, April). *Women's careers as a critique of the administrative culture.* Paper presented at the annual meeting of the American Educational Research Association, San Francisco.

Marshall, S. A., & Heller, M. (1983, August). A female leadership style could revolutionize school governance. *American School Board Journal,* pp. 31-32.

Martin, J. A., & Grant, G. P. (1990). Sex discrimination in West Virginia. *Principal, 70*(2), 40.

Matczynski, T. J., & Comer, K. C. (1991). *Mentoring women and minorities in higher education: An anecdotal record.* (ERIC Document Reproduction Services No. ED 331 376)

McCarthy, M., Kuh, G. D., Newell, L., & Iacona, C. M. (1988). *Under scrutiny: The educational administration professoriate.* Tempe, AZ: University Council for Educational Administration.

Mertz, N. T., & McNeely, S. R. (1990, April). *Getting to be a professor of educational administration: A study of how females "got" the job.* Paper presented at the annual meeting of the American Educational Research Association, Boston.

Metzger, C. (1985). Helping women prepare for principalships. *Phi Delta Kappan, 67*(4), 292-296.

Miller-Loessi, K. (1992). Toward gender integration in the workplace. *Sociological Perspective, 35*(1), 1-15.

Mims, N. G. (1992, November). *Can women aspiring to administrative positions break the glass ceiling?* Paper presented at the annual conference of the Southern Regional Council on Educational Administration, Atlanta, GA.

Missouri Department of Elementary and Secondary Education. (1994). *Current status report: Missouri educational administrators.* Jefferson City: Author.

Nadler, G., & Hibino, S. (1990). *Breakthrough thinking.* Rocklin, CA: Prima.

Newman, N. A. (1993, November). *Making it to the top: Results of structured interviews with women in university level administrative positions.* Paper presented at the annual meeting of the Mid-South Educational Research Association, New Orleans, LA.

News quotes: Women judges step up to the bench. (1994). *Women's VU, 17*(1), 3.

Patton, M. Q. (1987). *How to use qualitative methods in evaluation.* Newbury Park: Sage.

Pavan, B. N., & D'Angelo, J. M. (1990, April). *Gender differences in the career paths of aspiring and incumbent educational administrators.* Paper presented at the annual meeting of the American Educational Research Association, Boston.

Picker, A. (1980). Female educational administrators: Coping in a basically male environment. *Educational Horizons, 58*(3), 145-149.

Pigford, A. B., & Tonnsen, S. (1993). *Women in school leadership: Survival and advancement guidebook.* Lancaster, PA: Technomic.

Pines, M. (1980, December). Psychological hardiness: The role of challenge in health. *Psychology Today,* pp. 34-44, 98.

Porat, K. L. (1985, December). The woman in the principal's chair in Canada. *Phi Delta Kappan,* pp. 297-301.

Reagan, B. R. (1975). Two supply curves for economists? Implications of mobility and career attainment of women. *American Economic Review, 65*(2), 100-107.

Report reveals decline in college enrollment. (1994, July). *Higher Education and National Affairs,* p. 6.

Rist, M. C. (1991). Opening your own doors. *The Executive Educator, 13*(1), 14.

Roberts, S. V. (1992, April 27). Will 1992 be the year of the woman? *U.S. News and World Report,* pp. 37-39.

Rogus, J. F. (1988). Teacher leader programming: Theoretical under-pinnings. *Journal of Teacher Education, 39*(1), 46-52.

Sadker, M., & Sadker, D. (1993). *Failing at fairness: How America's schools cheat girls.* New York: McGraw-Hill.

Sadker, M., Sadker, D., & Klein, S. (1991). *Review of research in educa-tion.* Washington, DC: American Educational Research Associa-tion.

Sadler, B. R. (1978). *Sexual harassment* (Project on the Status and Edu-cation of Women, Association of American Colleges). Available from the Center for Women Policy Studies, Washington, DC.

Sagaria, M. A. (1988). *Empowering women: Leadership development strategies on campus.* San Francisco: Jossey-Bass.

Saldanha, L. (1988). *Information technology and the training and career development of women: The case of India* (Training Discussion Paper No. 30.) Geneva, Switzerland: International Labour Office.

Sandler, B. (1994). Important events in the history of sexual harass-ment in education. *About Women on Campus, Spring,* 6.

Sandroff, R. (1994, January). When women make more than men. *Working Woman,* pp. 38-41, 87.

Schwartz, P. (1994, August 18). Daddy's home. *The New York Times,* p. 4.

Schwartz, P. (1994). *Peer marriage: How love between equals really works.* New York: Free Press.

Scollay, S. (1994, April). The forgotten half. *American School Board Journal,* pp. 46-48.

Shakeshaft, C. (1989). *Women in educational administration.* Newbury Park, CA: Sage.

Shakeshaft, C., & Cohan, A. (1990, April). *In loco parentis: Sexual abuse in schools.* Paper presented at the annual meeting of the Ameri-can Educational Research Association, Boston.

Shrewsbury, C. M. (1987). What is feminist pedagogy? *Women's Stud-ies Quarterly, 15*(3), 6-14.

Stokes, M. J. (1984). *Organizational barriers and their impact on women in higher education.* Washington, DC: National Association for Women Deans, Administrators, and Counselors.

Swoboda, M. J., & Millar, S. B. (1986). Networking-mentoring: Ca-reer strategy of women in academic administration. *Journal of the National Association for Women Deans, Administrators, and Counselors, 50*(1), 8-12.

Tallerico, M., Burstyn, J. N., & Poole, W. (1993). *Gender and politics at work: Why women exit the superintendency.* Fairfax, VA: National Policy Board for Educational Administration.

Tannen, D. (1990). *You just don't understand: Women and men in conversation.* New York: William Morrow.

Taylor, A. (1984). Women as leaders. *Vital Speeches of the Day, 50*(14), 445-448.

Teitel, L., & O'Connor, K. (1993). Teachers as leaders: Implications for the preparation of principals. *Connections, 2*(1), 1, 6.

The 25 hottest careers. (1993, July). *Working Woman,* pp. 41-48.

Thomson, S. (Ed.). (1993). *Principals for our changing schools.* Fairfax, VA: National Policy Board for Educational Administration.

Tonnsen, S., Pigford, A., Jenkins, P., & Turner, N. (1992, November). *Training women leaders.* Paper presented at the Southern Regional Council on Educational Administration, Atlanta, GA.

"Tune Into Your Rights." (1985). Ann Arbor: University of Michigan, School of Education.

Turner, C. S., & Thompson, J. R. (1993). Socializing women doctoral students: Minority and majority experiences. *Review of Higher Education, 16*(3), 355-370.

U.S. Department of Education. (1992). *Strengthening support and recruitment of women and minorities to positions in education administration.* Washington, DC: Office of Educational Research and Improvement.

Valiant, S. (1978). *Women at work.* Princeton: New Jersey State Department of Education.

Weller, J. (1988). *Women in educational leadership* (Ohio State University Monograph). Columbus, OH: Center for Sex Equity.

Wolf, N. (1994). *Fire with fire.* New York: Random House.

Woo, C. (1985). Women administrators: Profiles of success. *Phi Delta Kappan,* pp. 285-287.

Yeakey, C. C., Johnston, G. S., & Adkison, J. A. (1986). In pursuit of equity: A review of research on minorities and women in educational administration. *Educational Administration Quarterly, 22*(3), 110-149.

Young, B. (1990, June). *Chance, choice, and opportunity in the careers of four women educators.* Paper presented at the annual meeting of the Canadian Society for Studies in Education, Victoria, BC.

Zweig, C. (1983, May). The eleventh megatrend. *Esquire,* pp. 99-138.

Suggested Readings

ATE at work: Gender equity, global education. (1994, July-August). *ATE Newsletter*, p. 2.

Barr, M., & Upcraft, M. L. (Eds.). (1988). *Empowering women: Leadership development strategies on campus.* San Francisco: Jossey-Bass.

Bruce, C. (1991, March). Mentorships essential for women in administration. *NASSP Newsleader*, p. 1.

Derrington, M. L. (1991). What it takes to be the superintendent's husband. *The Executive Educator, 13*(1), 13-14.

Grover, D. C. (1992). Women educators: Leadership in the 1990s. *Community/Junior College Quarterly, 16*(4), 329-343.

Huff, B. C. (1993). Clinton's health care plan faces important issues for women. *Women's VU, 16*(3), 7.

Jacobson, S. L. (1989). School management: Still a white man's game. *The Executive Educator, 11*(11), 19.

McGrath, S. T. (1992). Here come the women! *Educational Leadership, 49*(5), 62-65.

National Center for Education Statistics. (1994, January). *Public and private school principals: Are there too few women?* Washington, DC: U.S. Department of Education, Office of Educational Research and Improvement.

Shepard, S. (1994). *The status of women in rural Missouri.* Jefferson City: Missouri Department of Elementary and Secondary Education.

Tennessee State Department of Education. (1986). *Career ladder state model for local evaluation manual.* Nashville: Tennessee State Department of Education.

Tiedje, L., Wortman, C. B., Downer, G., Emmons, C., Biernat, M., & Lang, E. (1990). Women with multiple roles: Role compatibility perceptions, satisfaction, and mental health. *Journal of Marriage and the Family, 52*(1), 63-72.

Wheeler, B. (1993). Political correctness and the "feminization" of academe. *National Teaching and Learning Forum, 2*(6), 1-3.

Index

Aburdene, P., 5, 37, 38, 44, 45
Adkison, J. A., 15, 16, 20, 25
American Association of Colleges
    of Teacher Education, 27, 36
American Association of School
    Administrators, 19, 99, 106
American Association of Univer-
    sity Women, 15, 98, 108
American Council on Education, 36
Andrews, R. L., 47
Association of Teacher Education,
    36, 107
Astin, H. J., 75
Auel, J., 7

Barnett, B., 95
Barth, R., 89
Basom, M. R., 47
Blumberg, A., 89

Bolton, E., 77
Brathwaite, F., 16
Burstyn, J., 80

Caffarella, R., 95
Career paths, 1, 101-103
Castle Hot Springs Program, 91
Change, 51, 53
Cohan, A., 16
Cohorts, 94
Colleagiality, 90
Comer, K., 81
Commitment, 51, 52
Communication, 35
Courington, S., 51
Crosby, F., 33, 36

Daloz, L., 73

Danforth Foundation, 26
D'Angelo, J., 102, 104
Daresh, J. C., 75, 83, 86
Demographics, 18,
DePree, M., 46
DeSanctis, M., 89
Dopp, B. K., 21, 102, 104, 105, 106,
        110
Duvall, B., 97

East Tennessee State University,
        92
Edson, S. K., 10, 15
Eisler, R., 7
Erickson, K., 100

Fagenson, E., 75
Feistritzer, C., 110
Female Educators' Mentorship
        Project, 80
Feuer, D., 46
Financial savvy, 11, 59, 64, 65
Flax, E., 20
Fong, M. L., 33
Funk, C., 97

Gehrke, N. J., 81
Gender bias, 10, 107
Generational views, 30
Graduate school, 10, 25, 76, 94-96
Grant, G. P., 10
Grogan, A., 37
Guy, M., 28

Hagberg, J., 45
Hammond, L. A., 33
Hammons, J. O., 46
Heller, M., 87
Hennig, M., 75, 76
Hersi, D. T., 75

Hill, F. W., 6
Hill, M. S., 6, 23, 92, 95, 96
Human resources, 24

Iacona, C. M., 25
Integrated services, 24
Internal barriers, 15
Interviewees, 2-4,
Isolation, 13, 43, 77, 79, 88

Jardim, A., 75, 76
Jarvis, B., 52
Jenkins, P., 94
Job titles, 12
Johnson, J. R., 87
Johnston, G. S., 15, 16, 20, 25
Jones, E. H., 19

Kappa Delta Pi, 98
Karge, B. D., 89
Keller, L., 46
Kelly, R., 28
Keohane, N., 40, 78
Klein, S., 15
Kobasa, S. C., 51
Kosnett, J., 29
Kram, K. E., 73
Kuh, G. D., 25

Lawton, M., 28
Leadership preparation, 10. See also
        Graduate school
Leadership skills, 50, 55
Leadership studies, 45, 47
Leadership style, 47
Legislation, 40
Leisure, 98, 109
Leland, C., 75
Lieberman, A., 93
Locus of control, 52, 53

Lunenburg, F. C., 47
Luten, T., 79
Lynch, H., 80

Maddi, S., 51
Marshall, C., 10, 35
Marshall, S. A., 87
Martin, J. A., 10
Massachusetts Academy for Teachers, 93
Matcynski, T. J., 81
McCarthy, M., 25
McNeely, S., 76
Menopause, 38
Mentoring, 12, 13, 29, 72-86
Mentoring Association, 86
Mertz, N., 76
Metger, C., 91
Millar, S. B., 88
Miller-Loessi, K., 39
Mims, N., 10, 14
Minority women, 20
Missouri Department of Elementary and Secondary Education, 68
Mitchell, B., 10
Mobility, 13
Montenegro, X., 19
Motherhood, 28

Naisbitt, J., 5, 37, 38, 44, 45, 49
National Association of Secondary School Principals, 86
National Institute of Health, 37
National Policy Board for Educational Administration, 46, 49
Networking, 70, 71, 87-100
Newell, L., 25
Newman, N. A., 33, 34

O'Connor, K., 93

Ornstein, A. C., 47

Patton, M., 4
Pavan, B., 102, 104
Phi Delta Kappa, 98
Picker, A., 63
Pigford, A., 10, 94
Pines, M., 51
Pitner, N., 100
Playko, M. A., 75, 83, 86
Political savvy, 60
Politics, 10, 11, 16, 19, 29
Poole, W., 80
Porat, K., 69
Power feminism, 16
Principalship, 10, 65, 91

Queen bee syndrome, 78

Reagan, B. R., 14
Retirements, 18, 25
Rist, M., 99
Roberts, S. V., 19
Rogus, J. F., 94

Sadker, D., 15, 108
Sadker, M., 15, 108
Sagaria, M., 78
Salaries, 10, 18, 67, 68
Saldanha, L., 29
Sandroff, R., 14
Schwartz, P., 107
Scollay, S., 111
Sexual harassment, 107, 108
Shakeshaft, C., 16, 48, 104, 106
Shrewsbury, C. M., 95
Simmons, M., 92
Sloan, C. A., 21, 102, 104, 105, 106, 110
Stephens, G., 99

Stereotypes, 8, 28
Stokes, M. J., 15
Superintendency, 10, 11, 12, 22, 66,
     80, 105
Swoboda, M. J., 88

Tallerico, M., 80
Taylor, A., 35
Technology, 23, 29, 35, 92, 98, 99
Teitel, L., 93
Television images, 8
Thompson, J. R., 75
Thomson, S., 46, 49
Tokenism, 13,
Tonnsen, S., 10, 94
Turner, C. S., 75
Turner, N., 94
Turnovers, 18

United States Department of
     Education, 34, 91
University of South Carolina, 94

Valient, S., 7

Weller, J., 46
Western Michigan University, 86
Wolf, N., 16
The Women's Institute, 94
Woo, C., 63

Yeakey, C. C., 15, 16, 20, 25
Young, B., 79

Zweig, C., 49